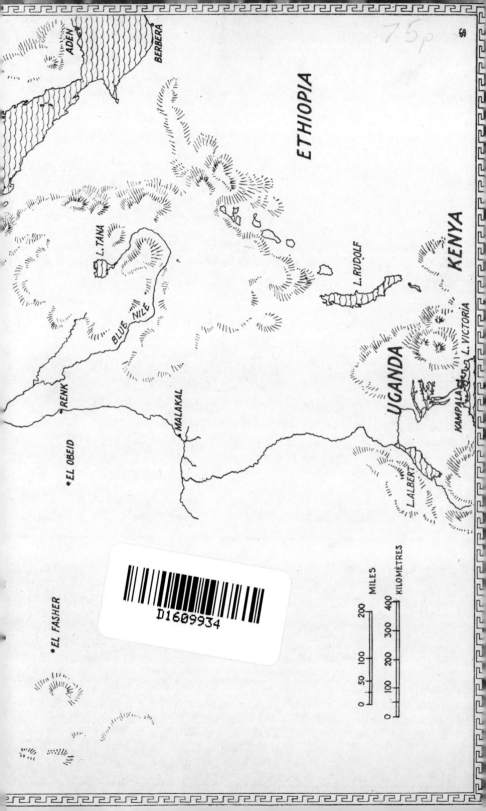

# A Talent for Trouble

# A Talent for Trouble

by

Ranulph Fiennes

HODDER AND STOUGHTON
LONDON   SYDNEY   AUKLAND   TORONTO

For Ginnie

# ACKNOWLEDGEMENTS

We are grateful to the following for their invaluable help before and during the expedition, without which the journey would not have been possible. In alphabetical order.

The Automobile Association
Sayyid Abu-Sunn, Sudanese Press Attaché in London
The Army Mapping Depot in Guildford
British Petroleum
British Berkefeld Filters
The British Ambassadors and their wives in Cairo and Khartoum
The British Commercial Attaché in Nairobi
John Blashford-Snell of the Scientific Exploration Society
Colonel Freddie de Butts in Cairo
The Cooper Motor Corporation of Nairobi
Colonel Eeles of the Hovercraft Directorate, M.O.T.
Colonel and Mrs. Nigel Crawford in Kampala
All at Hoverair Ltd.
Horlicks Ltd.
Brigadier Hussein Ali Karrar in Khartoum
Sir Khatim Al Khalifa
Sayyid Moyadeen and Sayyid Mubarreq in Wadi Halfa and the Commissioner of Wadi Halfa
Racal Electronics of Bracknell
R.F.D. Ltd.
The Rover Company
The Shell Companies of the Sudan and East Africa
Colonel and Mrs. Dick Tamplin of Khartoum
Townsend Ferries
Velocettes Ltd. (Perkins of Birmingham)

# CONTENTS

# ILLUSTRATIONS

All photographs in the book were taken by the author, owing to
the unfortunate accident which occurred to Michael Broome,
the professional photographer attached to the expedition, with
the exception of the photograph of the expedition before leaving
Dover, which is by courtesy of the *Daily Telegraph,* and the one
of unloading Baker, which was taken by Michael Broome.

## MAPS

# FOREWORD

## by Lieut. Colonel Colin Mitchell, M.P.

Courage and enterprise often go together and the author of this book has his fair share of both qualities. Captain Sir Ranulph Twisleton-Wykeham-Fiennes lives up to his family motto, 'Look for a brave spirit'.

The story of the Hovercraft, that splendid British invention, has been told elsewhere. Frustration and disappointment dogged those far-sighted few who saw in the concept unlimited possibilities; a revolutionary breakthrough for travel and communications methods on land and water. The Nile enterprise, which this book describes, made a positive contribution to the export and sale of these modern craft by proving their reliability under testing conditions of terrain and climate.

Apart from the technical triumph and more material considerations, the expedition highlighted the spirit of enterprise which is still part of our British heritage. The author is in the tradition of Army officers who ache for travel and adventure during the dull routine of peacetime soldiering. In the past it was easier to find suitable outlets for these restless spirits than it is today, when bureaucratic military control dominates to the ends of the earth. This book proves, refreshingly, that even if the adventures are becoming rarer the species is still very much alive—even fully mechanised!

To young men and women who complain that opportunities for real-life travel and excitement are diminishing the lesson is clear—opportunity awaits anyone with the courage and determination to create it.

COLIN MITCHELL

# CHAPTER 1

∞

## The Travel Bug

Britain in the late nineteen-sixties saw four young men in an assortment of rowing boats fight their way over the wild Atlantic; a bearded sailor circumnavigated the world non-stop, and a little group of scientists trudged over a world of broken ice: two rubber dinghies penetrated the hitherto unnavigated gorges of the Upper Blue Nile and a giant hovercraft blazed new trails in the heart of Brazil.

Britain's small army of private explorers and adventurers followed their migratory urges in different ways to every corner of the world. The Union Jack may have drooped as sterling slumped and the world shook its head at the lack of drive in a nation so recently proud and successful; but the flag flapped in a friendly breeze of international acclaim as Francis Chichester and Alec Rose rounded Plymouth Hoe.

The desire to travel in strange regions, to get away from congested urban life, to pit themselves against the elements and to test their individual endurance to the utmost are some of the varied reasons which drive these pioneers. They are also intrigued to test novel ways of travel, to experiment with new methods, new machines, new gear, or to re-assess old techniques in the light of new knowledge. Achievement is their reward and persistence their characteristic. If there was enough money to be had in expeditions most of them would become perpetual professional travellers and explorers.

I too have always wanted to explore and for this reason joined the Army; a profession which would enable me to do this from time to time, and to see new places and people. I have parachuted into Norway, canoed in Germany, walked the Pyrenees, fought in Southern Arabia; seen the Empty Quarter and prowled the African veld. But most of all I have always wanted to ascend the Nile.

The Nile has always fascinated me and in the modern tradition of travel I longed to prove an untried machine against this most ancient of rivers. Finally in the spring of 1969 I managed to accomplish my aim by taking up the Nile two very small hovercraft which had previously only travelled for four miles at a time round a Lincolnshire gravel-pit.

An avid reader of travel books, I am interested not only in what the pioneers did and what they accomplished, but in the people themselves. Why did Robin Knox-Johnston survive his sail round the world whilst Donald Crowhurst broke down? What enabled Wilfred Thesiger to keep going through the extremes of the Empty Quarter? I always long to know more about the writers' backgrounds, how they came to travel in the first place, what inspired them and often feel that if only I knew a little more about them, it would help me to build up a better picture.

Because this has always interested me personally and in case there are others of a like mind who like to know more about a traveller than just his tale, I feel it behoves me to give a brief outline first of how I came to go down the Nile, what experiences I had had beforehand and what the problems were which had to be faced in planning the expedition. Moreover some of the wilder episodes in my past had considerable bearing on what happened.

I have had the travel bug for as long as I can remember. Perhaps a nomadic youth encouraged me, for I spent the first ten months of my life being moved around in the South of England as the Germans altered the areas of their bombing and doodlebugging. Then I moved to South Africa soon after the end of the Second World War, my father having died of wounds in Italy. My playmates in South Africa were the local coloured kids, and at eight or nine years old I found great pleasure in joining them in long rambles through the rolling vine plantations and dark pine-woods of Tokai Forest where young baboons cried and packs of wild dogs roamed the glades.

After schooling in the Cape and later in England, with the occasional skiing holiday as an introduction to Europe, I decided to join my father's old regiment, the Scots Greys, for by then I had recognised a driving urge: to travel and see all that was possible. So I was easily hooked by the 'Join the Army and See the World' delusion.

After training at Mons Officer Cadet School and the armoured gunnery and signals centres, there was a period of two months leave before being sent to Germany to join the Scots Greys regiment out there. Two months in which to travel, so I decided to cross the Anatolian Desert in southern Turkey which looked on the map to be wild and remote. Camel loads were worked out, Bulgarian and Albanian transit visas obtained, and injections suffered; but two weeks before the 'off', the Army stepped in. Turkey had become 'temporarily delicate' and not an area where British soldiers should be allowed even on leave. A quick change of plan and destination found us crossing the Pyrenees by mule: a pleasant enough journey but a poor second best to the Turkish idea.

Much of the next four years was spent in the grimy interiors of Centurion tanks thundering across the bleak plains of northern Germany 'perfecting the armoured withdrawal'. NATO planners must be of a very practical, or possibly realistic, frame of mind for we spent little time advancing. I quickly made up my mind to escape from the interminable months of churned-up mud and greasy denim overalls as soon as was possible. This turned out to be fairly easy for the regiment had large canoeing and skiing teams with, at the time, no one to look after them. I was lucky enough to be given both jobs and each successive year spent two summer months paddling down the main rivers of Europe and the three winter months 'langlauf' or cross-country skiing in the Bavarian Alps with a team of (temporarily) very fit Jocks. One leave, with a civilian friend and a girl, I tried to cross Norway from Bergen to Oslo by canoe. The attempt nearly ended in disaster for the canoes were dashed to pieces before we had completed half the journey; but I felt there was immense scope for interesting travel in central Norway and decided to revisit the glacial rivers of the Jotunheim district at the next opportunity with more time and better equipment.

So in the summer of 1967, I contacted four friends and we agreed to visit the Jostedalsbre. This is a vast glacial plateau in central Norway of three hundred square miles of ice with a thin snow covering, laced with crevasses and punctured by 6,000 foot peaks. It is Europe's largest and most forbidding glacier.

Instead of driving north of Bergen in a car and then facing a fearsome climb onto the glacier heavily laden with packs, we decided to drop by parachute with all our kit from a seaplane and then, once on the Jostedalsbre, to follow by ski and canoe what was thought to be the route of the ancient Viking peoples over the glacier and down the glacial rivers and inland lakes to the sea. The five of us would all require parachute training. I received mine at the French Freefall School in the Pyrenees, which was a bad mistake, for I found that my French, which had once been quite respectable, had been forgotten and anyway the garbled military slang of the para instructors was far beyond my ken. The direct result of this was my first jump being made in a state of almost complete ignorance. The chute had opened, but on looking up I saw to my horror that instead of a methodical series of rigging lines stretching away to the canopy, there was a tangled line which ended in a knot behind my neck. This was 'les twistes' I learnt later and is a common malfunction resulting usually from a poor jumping position. The drill for this had been explained but I had obviously not understood; as it was, the laws of elasticity saw me out of my troubles by spinning me round and round—I was still spinning when I hit the ground. The instructor, who had witnessed all, was not impressed and although I couldn't understand his comments, my fellow first-jumpers, who were all French, seemed to find them uproariously funny and slapped my already uncomfortable back.

The course had ended in a night jump, and I was quite sure the instructor had also mentioned a water landing. This was perfectly in order, since there was a lake on the dropping zone, and we had been carefully instructed in 'wet landings'.

However, I was surprised that no life-belts were issued on

With my Recce Section on the fringes of the Empty Quarter.

The expedition before it left Dover. *From left to right:* Anthony Brockhouse, self, Charles Westmorland, Nick Holder, Mike Broome and Peter Loyd.

Atlantis of the Nubian Desert — the Commissioner of Wadi Halfa shows the author his murals which depict the town and oasis as it was before being totally submerged as a result of the construction of the Aswan Dam.

Baker and Burton stop for a midday rest above the Second Cataract.

boarding the Nord Atlas troop plane that night. Later on, floating gently downwards in the dark, I thought I could perceive the whitish shade of what was obviously the lake approaching. I banged the catch of the safety harness, and slipped out of the crutch straps. Hanging now to the chute harness only by my armstraps, I noticed at the last moment that the white shade was a sort of ground mist and that the landing was to be as solid as ever. Fortunately the instructor could not see the disastrous landing which followed, or I feel I would have foregone the honour of the Wings with which I was presented next day: big metal ones which were also attached to the battle-dress of some eighty cadets over their proudly puffed French chests. The Norweigian glacier landing, when it came, was far more comfortable than any of my French landings.

The Jostedalsbre journey took two weeks and all went well. No-one was killed, although Peter Loyd, a helicopter pilot and experienced free-faller, landed some few feet from the lips of a yawning crevasse. As on the earlier attempt, however, the canoes could not stand up to the racing rocky rivers and were reduced to matchwood by the rapids.

Later on in 1967, back in Germany after the Norwegian expedition, a letter came from a major in the Scots Greys who for the last two years had been posted to the Sultan of Muscat's Armed Forces in the little known lands of Oman. The Sultan (deposed by his son Qabus bin Said in July 1970) liked his Army to be partly officered by English soldiers who were seconded from their regiments to do this. In return the R.A.F. were allowed to use Masira and Salalah as bases. The major said that the Sultan's Forces were always ready to accept new officers; it was simply a matter of putting in an application. Glancing out of the window at the grey German skies and muddy plain, a horizon broken only by rashes of stunted fir and the barbed wire of the garrison fence, I re-read the letter and applied. A month later my application was answered with a summons to a three month course in Arabic at the Army School of Education at Beaconsfield. There Arabic is taught to those about to depart for service in the Middle East where rich rulers still entrust their little armies to British 'advisers'.

B

## A Talent For Trouble

The Arabic course was enjoyable, for the evenings and weekends were free and the West End only half an hour's drive away. Arabic homework was therefore usually sacrificed for the joys of life which were reported to be unobtainable in the Oman. Three months in which to secure lascivious memories sufficient for two years in the wilderness. Three months, too, in which to plan an expedition in the Middle East for, once out there, it would be a wonderful opportunity to use my leave for exploring some wild part of Africa or Arabia.

Nick Holder, who had parachuted with us into Norway, was now a civilian selling razor-blades to the Arabs in the Persian Gulf countries—the most confirmed of beard-wearers. He was based in Bahrein and had written to me with a number of suggestions for possible journeys. He sent me a copy of Alan Moorehead's *The White Nile*. I read it twice and was doubly fascinated by the unique character of this almost human river, rich in history and cutting through 4,000 miles of Egypt, the Sudan and Uganda. Nick pointed out that only one hundred years ago the greatest of Britain's explorers were making their names and history with their epic journeys into the perilous regions which till then had defied all efforts to find the source of the longest river in the world. A hundred years since such controversial characters as Sir Richard Burton, Speke and Grant, Livingstone, the amazing Stanley and that idol of the eighteen-seventies, Samuel Baker, had made the world reverberate with their accounts of the African interior. Why not mark the centenary of these men by an expedition into the area of their toils? Why should we not ascend the Nile as a memorial to our adventurous forebears of the eighteen-seventies?

Of course, in the hundred odd years that have elapsed since Sir Samuel and Lady Baker made their journey to discover Lake Albert, conditions have undergone considerable changes in the lands bordering the river. Well pot-holed tarmac roads exist in much of the United Arab Republic (as Egypt is now called) and Uganda; and in the Sudan, mud tracks follow the river for much of its course. Hostile tribesmen are no longer expected to attack passing travellers, and even the Sudd, that great barrier of swamp in southern Sudan, has been mapped with a fair degree

of accuracy. But obstacles of quite a different nature have arisen
to-day with which the Bakers and their fellow-travellers did not
have to contend. In their day, ninety-eight per cent of the
territory on both banks lay under the influence of British official-
dom or friendly Arab dealers. A British passport to-day no
longer moves mountains in the Sudan or Egypt. Deep suspicion
is aroused in both countries by the European, whether Welsh or
Sicilian, whose desire to photograph anything of interest is in
direct opposition to the dictates of the security conscious police
and army authorities. Now very few Europeans are permitted to
ascend the errant course of the Nile even as tourists and certainly
not by private vehicle along its banks; those that have made the
journey by rail or river ferry have had their view, along with their
insight of the country and its peoples, curtailed by either bank.

Since the Six Day War of 1967, Egypt and Israel have virtually
been at war continuously and the Nile forms a rear defence line.
This political situation has made the random traveller in Egypt,
not unnaturally, unwelcome from a security point of view. The
Sudan, too, has had her internal revolutions and as a result is
quite rightly very security conscious. Although package and
steamer tours are tolerated because they are easily kept under
official surveillance, the lone tourist or small group of wandering
travellers, whose movements are not necessarily predictable, and
whose safety in the more remote areas cannot be guaranteed,
are not normally permitted. To-day's Nile traveller may see the
occasional Coca Cola sign even in the most remote village of
the Sudd, but he can comfort himself in the knowledge that only
a select few have managed to complete the journey from
beginning to end. Political problems both external and internal
and the ever encroaching communist menace are not improving
prospects of others who wish to try. Now, as I write this in 1970,
the journey is no longer possible, nor is it likely to be allowed
within the foreseeable future.

However, back in 1968, a journey up the Nile did seem to be
possible even if beset with problems, so I decided to do some
research into the difficulties whilst on the London course in
Arabic. First, visits to the three embassies involved, that of the
U.A.R., and those of the Sudan and Uganda. On the surface

there appeared to be no unsurmountable hurdles, no reason why we should not be granted visas though no guarantee that we would. There were various possible methods of travel, of which Land-Rover seemed the most likely, and it seemed that it would take nearly a year to get organised. I would be due six weeks leave in the spring of 1969. Peter Loyd and Nick Holder were both keen to come and so I suggested that they put in early bids for leave at this time with their employers.

However, February 1969 was not a good time to choose from the point of view of the weather. The vicious 'haboob' sand-storms of the Nubian desert usually begin in mid-March and by all accounts would render travel through the sand, even in Land-Rovers, virtually impossible. Again, south of Khartoum, and especially between Malakal and Juba, the high flood season lasts for seven months during which period, the 'sudd' swamps cover an area larger than Great Britain. These rains usually, during a normal year, begin in April. On a rough schedule, therefore, we would have to be just about clear and south of the flood regions by the end of March which was cutting things a bit fine and not leaving much margin for error.

Another problem which we had to take into consideration was that of Lake Nasser, the 200-mile long reservoir caused by the Aswan Dam. The lake water was still rising and had not yet reached its final level so there were no maps of its coastline yet made and all the old roads and tracks which ran alongside had long since been wiped out. The rising flood water had covered complete townships and drowned many ancient villages. This had caused great ill-feeling among the local people and there had been much local unrest during the preceding years.

Just when we thought we had assessed all the problems which we would meet with in Egypt and were thinking of ways to surmount them, the Egyptians became very concerned over an ambiguous speech made by the British Defence Minister of the time, which indicated that a substantial arms deal with the Israelis might well be on the cards and might take place at any time. Should such an arrangement be made before our expedition, we would certainly never get our U.A.R. visas; should it occur whilst we were actually passing through Egypt, the chances of our getting out again would be remote. Should the Israelis attack across the Suez Canal and force the Egyptian forces to make a last ditch stand along the Nile, we would indeed be in jeopardy. As the possibility of the Nile being a line of defence loomed larger, security in its immediate vicinity became more important to the Egyptian army, police and homeguard.

Next we had to look at the problems posed by the Sudan. Although the Sudanese contributed a fair number of troops and essential equipment to the Arab war effort, the action is too far from their own territory to have much effect on Sudanese civilians. But they have their own troubles, for the south of the country is inhabited by numerous native tribes who are no more Sudanese in origin than the Ugandans. Those who are not pagans had Christian instruction during the years of British rule and so they have naturally a very reasonable objection to being ruled by Arab Muslims from far away Khartoum. Many of the Southern Sudanese would like to be independent and some of the offiicials in Khartoum blame this urge for regional independence on the British, who, they say, encouraged such feelings when they were in occupation. Whatever the reasons for discontent, and they are many, there is a strong element of the southern Sudanese populace who, since early 1955, have given vent to their feelings through active rebellion of a guerilla nature and although much of their activity is now confined to the Equatorial Province and the forest regions to the west of the Nile, road ambushes with sabotage of bridges and defiles are still fairly common to the south of Bor. Rebels are liable to attack without warning from out of the forest armed with razor-sharp spears of local manufacture or Czech machine-guns from foreign supporters.

So much for the Sudan. How about Uganda? What sort of complications were we likely to meet there?

The Ugandan problems were really an extension of those in the Sudan, for the Ugandans had clandestinely allowed, over the years, large groups of these Christian Sudanese rebels—known as the Anya Nya—to come over their border in the hill country east of Nimule and take sanctuary. For it was widely reported that these Christian communities were being heavily persecuted by the Sudanese Government.

These border incursions, not publically admitted by the Ugandans, led to occasional trespass by the pursuing Sudanese troops into Ugandan territory as they tried to capture or shoot their rebellious subjects. Some months earlier a lorry load of Sudanese troops had been fired upon in error at a border crossing-point and some Ugandans were killed in the ensuing confusion. The border had been temporarily closed to all traffic while the governments attempted to sort things out. But feelings still ran high and the border might be closed again at any time. An unpleasant possibility, for even if we might successfully ascend the river's course through Egypt and Sudan, it would still be on the cards to find the journey halted at the Ugandan border, caught in a cul de sac with the Sudd flood rising behind us, no point of egress and neither the time, the money nor the visas for a return trip.

But then there is seldom much good to be had from viewing things solely from the pessimistic point of view and the more I learnt of the Nile lands, the greater became their attraction. If we could obtain visas to all the countries then we could surmount the political problems; if we started in good time we would be able to overcome the wind, rain and weather complications. If we chose an ingenious method of travel we might overcome the lack of roads round Lake Nasser and also the problems of rising flood water and haboob sandstorms.

The next thing to be done was to obtain equipment. Neither Peter, Nick nor I were prepared or able to dig deep into bottomless pockets to finance such a long journey. We must therefore try to make the journey self-financing. Our kit for the Norwegian journey had either been lent by the army or had been loaned by private firms in order to demonstrate their product or test its endurance. Both Horlicks and Tyne Folding Boats had been particularly helpful.

Before they were taken over by the Beecham Group, Horlicks produced a range of concentrated ration packs which could be fitted into a pocket and yet were highly nutritious and specially prepared for the needs of individual expeditions, bearing in mind extremes of climate and the possibility that non-pork-eating Muslim guides might well have to share the same rations. I therefore approached Horlicks again and Sir John Horlick kindly agreed to supply us free with some 380 pounds of rations for the Nile trip specially prepared by his calory expert Dr. de Jong, together with a much appreciated cash contribution towards our other expenses.

They also sent large supplies of pamphlets with exporting details and the promise that our rations would be delivered shortly before our departure. They commissioned us to write a report on the effects of a prolonged Horlicks diet under the climatic conditions and stresses of the Nile countries. We had intended to do this with the rations they prepared for our earlier Norwegian glacier journey, but a canoe carrying most of the packs had capsized and sunk in rapids. The rest of the packs had been lost when Nicholas slipped into a crevasse and became jammed therein by his rucksack. Only by consigning the pack and its Horlicks contents to posterity in the depths of the crevasse, did we manage to heave him out of his icy predicament.

I met an affable Pole who sold two-way radios for the British Communications Company who said that he would do all he could to persuade his bosses that a loan of three B.B.C. sets to our Nile expedition would do the Company nothing but good. They did not agree. But as luck would have it, the firm was taken over by Racal Electronics of Bracknell who had an adventurous sales manager with no objections to loaning equipment to 'sales promotion expeditions'. So we received three excellent Squadpack radios with frequencies chosen and pre-set to fit in with the regulations of the Nile countries and which would not enable us to chat with Israelis over the way.

Maps too, were obtained in great number and detail: my copy of the swamp regions alone, when the map sections were attached to one another end to end, was over twelve yards in length. These came from an Army map depot which did not seem to mind our lack of official military sponsorship. Vehicle spares, tools, crash helmets, radio fuses and a hundred other minor items of possible importance could all be obtained from Army stores so long as they were eventually returned from whence they came.

One of the most useful, efficient and popular gadgets was a water steriliser to deal with the notorious bugs of the Nile and its tributaries. These were loaned by British Berkefeld Filters; a big one for communal meals and six pocket-sized versions for filling individual water bottles. Where for pacification of irate tribesmen early explorers had used beads and cloth, we later found that these little water filters had a remarkable effect; so much so that we soon had none left and were ourselves reduced to drinking neat Nile water by the time we left the Sudan behind us.

Arms and ammunition hardly seemed necessary, but after hearing hair-raising stories of attacks by brigands and crocodiles on a recent journey down the Blue Nile, I felt it would be better to be safe than sorry, even at the certain risk of accusation of being melodramatic by the others. I had earlier been advised to take both an automatic and a 7.62 rifle with me to Muscat and had already purchased them in London; they should be sufficient for the Nile journey and I didn't envisage any difficulties borrowing ammunition from the Sultan's Forces.

By now we had decided to proceed in Land-Rovers and were presuming that the Army would lend them to us. We were fairly sure that Army aid would be forthcoming even if it had not yet been offered, for journeys of an original nature are usually encouraged for their testing of initiative and are often given loans of equipment and, from time to time, even money.

Unfortunately, however, when approached, the Army saw fit to remember my past and the Ministry of Defence decided that my personal history and records did nothing to encourage them in the wish to increase my initiative. Those people who mattered saw no reason for allowing two British khaki Land-Rovers to ascend the Nile defences for some 3,000 miles with me in charge. For in 1966 the Army Board had seen fit to remove me from the 22nd Special Air Service Regiment in which I was serving, and after a probationary period with the 14th/20th Hussars, an excellent regiment, I was eventually returned to the Greys.

The incident which caused this upheaval to an otherwise flourishing, though singularly unbrilliant, career, started in the

Wiltshire village of Upper Swainswick. A friend of mine from
earlier days at a Brighton language crammer's, then engaged in
selling French wines to the hotels of southern England, had
leased a charming cottage on Swainswick hill. Whilst testing
other brands in a nearby village pub he overheard the locals
complaining bitterly of the high-handed methods of the council
and the 'Americans'. It transpired that 20th Century Fox and all
its trappings had descended on the village: 'Dr Doolittle' with
Rex Harrison and Samantha Eggar was to be filmed on location
there, the trout stream dammed, concrete fronts erected and an
artificial lake provided. It appeared that although the Parish
Council had been consulted, the villagers hadn't, and apart from
a few who were making a quiet mint out of the arrival of the
'Americans', they objected strongly both to the invasion of their
privacy and to the apparent ruination of the unique quality of
their village. The fact that these same Americans had earlier
voted the village of Castle Combe to be Britain's Prettiest
Village only served to aggravate the matter.

My friend immediately felt personally involved: once again
the cause of 'mass entertainment' was riding roughshod over
the feelings of individuals. He telephoned me one week and
with three or four companions a plan was debated in his
Chelsea flat, the purpose of which was to bring to the public eye
the plight of the villagers of Castle Combe and expose the
high-handed methods of the moguls.

Rex and Samantha were due to arrive in the village one
Monday morning to begin filming the 'pondside sequences'. The
night before, after an excellent dinner in Bath, we arrived in
the village at 11 p.m. having made our way over the last two
miles on foot. The cars were left in a pub car park on the main
Chippenham-London road. Carrying quantities of explosives
and various fusing devices in haversacks we entered the spacious
gardens of what appeared to be the local manor and laid a
series of staggered time fuses, all attached to plastic explosive
flare balls. Most were among the cabbages and the manure heap;
one was on the gravel path behind a stone outhouse.

Local youths had been caught tampering with the film props
and with the sandbag dam itself, so Fox had called in Securicor

To Dear Jan,

With very many thanks for much appreciated hospitality and kindness.

with love from Ran.

with their Alsatians in order to guard the dam and props against further such attentions. That Sunday night it was obviously particularly important that nothing should happen: no dam meant no Puddleby-on-the-Marsh and therefore expensive delays to the tightly scheduled filming.

Our decoy flares were so positioned as to make it appear to anyone in the area of the dam that the garden containing all the film props, further up the village, was on fire. The flares were set at ten-minute intervals and one of our number had been left to observe the movement around the dam. Having lit the fuses, we joined him by a circuitous route. He affirmed that the dam was clear of 'the opposition' who had gone off to inspect the first flare, and we moved in to demolish the sandbags.

As I set foot on the dam top a growl and movement on the far bank announced the presence of the law—the pure brand, not just Securicor minions—and flight ensued. One of our number, shortsighted and bespectacled, hoofed his way myopically down the main lane and a fleet-footed policeman flagged him down with a blinding torch beam in the manner of a moth-collector making a catch. The others separated and fled in various directions; two of them only to be caught three days later back in Chelsea. I entered the trout stream and silently waded through the reeds for some hundreds of yards before climbing the bank and returning through a wood to the pub car park.

We had earlier contacted a freelance photographer, a T.A. trooper who had allegedly 'discovered' Jean Shrimpton before David Bailey did; he had been told that should he go to Castle Combe that night and await developments, he would get some very newsworthy photographs and a story which would 'fetch a packet with the dailies the next day'. In this manner we would ensure that the chaos for the Fox-men on the following day would not be hushed up. Reporters would descend on the village in a witch hunt for the identity of the unknown dambreakers and would in the process disclose to the nation the true feelings of the majority of the village towards the film-men.

As in all the best-laid plans; there was an unsuspected fly in the ointment. The freelance decided he would make far more money by disclosing the whole 'happening' to the papers and police before it took place. In the furtherance of his plans he followed our movements from Bath to the car park and after our departure overland flattened the tyres of the cars.

Therefore on my eventual return, dripping wet, to the car, a passing mini-van containing two policemen and their outsize hound observed my strange appearance and it was not long before I joined my myopic friend in the cells of Chippenham jail.

The judge at Salisbury Assizes next October found 'the use of explosives' to further our aims 'indefensible' and fined us a total of nine hundred pounds. He also stated his hope that 'our employers would regard the Court Order as a sufficient penalty'. Nevertheless the Army Board thereafter regarded me as 'to be watched'. Not the sort of person to be let loose with army equipment in areas as inflammable as the U.A.R. and Southern Sudan. I saw their point but was all the same perturbed to learn that absolutely no M.O.D. or Foreign Office aid could be extended to our journey or its preparation, which included the vital Land-Rovers.

Nick Holder had meanwhile found a possible source of revenue in a Bursary grant from the Eyre and Spottiswode Fund. We put up an appealing case for our project but it was turned down; as were three other attempts at obtaining financial sponsorship from various public spirited organisations. Similarly, although several firms were willing to lend us equipment to demonstrate in Cairo, Khartoum, Kampala and any other cities where sales of their wares might be effected, they were not willing to give us any agents' fees should our sales-drive produce successful results.

Giving up the unequal struggle to get funds, I concentrated on attempting to persuade the ambassadors from Egypt and the Sudan, and the High Commissioners from Kenya and Uganda to help with visas and other very necessary formalities. Each successive frontier would be an obstacle; for V.H.F. radios, automatic weapons, ammunition and an assortment of photographic equipment, as well as currency and vehicles, all needed a host of specially applied for documents. Written permission to motor through Egypt and certain parts of Northern Sudan was hard to get; for the south of Sudan—well-nigh impossible.

## A Talent For Trouble

The Sudanese Embassy is next door to St. James's Palace and I came to know it very well, for obtaining an interview with His Excellency was a matter of intricacy and patience. I had first to see—on different occasions—the Visa Section, the Commercial Attaché, the Press Attaché and the Military Attaché. All gave me numerous very good reasons for the undesirability of tourists wandering around Southern Sudan at the present time. The Egyptian Ambassador would not see me at all and the furthest I got was the Commercial Attaché, one Mustapha Hamdi. He was a pleasant man with an overpowering addiction to complete lack of ventilation in his office and to smoking unbroken chains of Gaulloise's most odorous brand: a mesmerising combination. We had long conversations and he was politely noncommittal over my spasmodic attempts at snappy rejoinders in Arabic. But I never got a paper out of him, much less a promise that all would be well with the journey. The Kenyan High Commissioner was refreshingly get-at-able, but as unconstructive in his advice as the others. His counterpart from Uganda was a charming man whose five year old daughter was playing dominoes on the carpet in his sumptuous office. He was extremely helpful, wrote me a number of addresses which I should contact in order to obtain the necessary travel papers, and suggested that the only trouble we might have was at the Nimule border post with the customs officials, who were in the habit of demanding cash deposits for thirty per cent of the value of all vehicles and new equipment from tourists, with the doubtful comment that it could be reclaimed later on one's way out of the country.

After some two dozen trips to London, I was still without visible proof of progress, and realised that with absolutely no strings to pull, it seemed unlikely that I could complete the necessary paperwork before the Arabic course ended and I had to leave for Muscat. A new approach was needed; something which could be used as a bait to tempt the ambassadors from their inertia and disinterest towards the Nile journey.

An earlier suggestion I had made to Nick Holder, and one which he had quite rightly turned down as being impractical, had been the crossing of Africa from Lake Chad to the east coast in two mini-hovercraft supported by a Land-Rover party. Initial

28

enquiries into the availability of small hovercraft had drawn so
complete a blank that I had given up the idea. But recently
Nick had come across an article about a five-seater hover vehicle
which could be adapted to spray crops. It was built experi-
mentally by some pottering pioneer and then bought up with
copyright by the giant Hovermarine Ltd. It sounded thoroughly
reliable and, although only a prototype had by then been made
and tested, it occurred to me that both the Egyptians and the
Sudanese, with their vast cotton crops to be sprayed, might well
be interested to see this revolutionary craft at work in their
respective countries. A hovercraft would not be affected by Nile
flooding nor by monsoon rains, nor would it then matter that
there were no roads round Lake Nasser. Moreover it would be a
great technological feat. The very idea of it might intrigue people
and make visas and papers easier to get hold of.

A visit to Hovermarine Ltd. in Southampton and discussions
with their sales representative eventually produced a letter from
them stating that, although they were extremely reluctant to
withdraw from the proposed expedition in 1969, the time factor
was too close for comfort in view of the untried nature of the
present Hovercat and that they would most certainly be
interested in co-operating with this expedition if it could be
delayed until 1970. This amounted to a dead-end for the journey
must be 1969 or never. In fact just before we set out, we heard
that a fire had burnt down much of the Hovermarine production
line and that the only available Hovercat had been reduced to
ashes.

The next port of call was the little known firm of Hoverair Ltd.
in Crowland, Lincolnshire. This was then owned and run by the
Brassey family and dominated by the amazing Lady Brassey.
In the middle of the nineteenth century the Brasseys had first
made a name for themselves in the field of travel. A Lord and
Lady Brassey had been round the world in the yacht *Sunbeam;*
a rare feat in those days. Sir Thomas Brassey had designed the
Victoria Bridge in Montreal, and most of the difficult engineering
problems of the Great Eastern Railway and Canadian Pacific were
solved by his ingenuity. In April 1966 the present Lady Brassey's
husband had bought a small circular hover machine to raise

cash for his local church fund. He then started a firm—Hoverair
—and by that same summer was taking his machines to boat, air,
and even motor shows. He died that autumn, but Lady Brassey
persevered and by the end of May 1968 a magnificent little
craft—the HA5 Hoverhawk—had been produced which was
demonstrated successfully at the international boat show and
the Geneva Motor Show soon after its debut.

Export orders followed from the most improbable countries
and firms for, with a simple spray attachment, the Hoverhawk
will spray crops cheaply and efficiently in places where wheeled
and tracked vehicles would sink. Shell even has one for examin-
ing its Kenyan offshore oil-rigs. Mexico, Zambia and Australia
are among the many countries to have bought these versatile
little craft for a wide variety of purposes.

We were met on arrival at Hoverair by a splendidly vague
man in overalls smelling strongly of resin and fresh sawdust.
Lady Brassey was apparently showing a prospective buyer the
craft in action on a nearby quarry pond, but she would be
lunching at the Ruddy Duck pub close by the pond and would
doubtless be delighted to hear of our project. We joined her at
the pub. She was entranced with the idea of two of her Hoverhawks mounting the Nile, and at once saw my point about the
Sudanese and U.A.R. cotton crops. We left with the impression
that the Hoverair 'board' would be sitting to decide if the scheme
was financially favourable to them. If so, we could go ahead.

With what I hoped would be two Hoverhawks to add to the
as yet mythical Land-Rovers, a large fuel problem was evident.
For the Hoverhawks could only carry six gallons of two-stroke
fuel on which they could run at full throttle for some two and a
half hours. The fuel stations along the Nile would be too far
apart for them and, if they were loaded down with drums of
petrol, they would never be able to get off the ground. So I would
have to take Land-Rovers along to carry the Hoverhawks' fuel
and these Land-Rovers would also have to be fuelled themselves.
Initial overtures to Shell were redirected to B.P. and after
several meetings with the latter's Sales Director and their hovercraft adviser Doug Hammet, it became clear that the hovercraft
industry as a whole was very heavily tied up with the Ministry

of Technology. M.O.T. had formed a Hovercraft Directorate Branch, and B.P. advised me to contact Colonel Eeles of the Directorate. If the colonel were to inspect the Hawk and find it reliable to the extent that it stood a good chance of surviving the rigours of the Nile, then B.P. would look after our refuelling problems.

I drove up to the quarry again, this time with Colonel Eeles. The vague foreman of my earlier visit had left the firm and a new sense of purpose seemed to pervade in the cramped little factory—a breakthrough had been achieved in the design, and although the queer looking machine seemed unchanged to me, Lady Brassey took us down to the launching area with pride and soon had the craft whirling and skidding round the confined space of the pond at alarming, but highly impressive, speeds. I took the controls gingerly at first, for they are quite unlike that of a car, motor boat or even aeroplane. Corners are taken in much the same way as a racing driver would take an icy bend, and since the quarry pond was both small and circular, bushes, mudbanks and reeds flashed by and I found myself forgetting just which point of the self-induced skid I had reached in relation to the banks. Panic ensued: I didn't actually crash but the steering went haywire, the engines revved violently without effecting the volition, and I came in to 'land' by luck more than by management. Lady B, on the bank, had naturally been having kittens but no damage was done and my own feelings were that the powerful little machines were just what we needed to get the Nile journey off its feet.

The surprising fact we had to face was that neither the Hover-hawk nor any other small hovercraft had, to Mintech's knowledge, ever driven farther than three or four miles non-stop, and although we had had the Hawk carefully tested by Mintech with a full simulated load and all engines at maximum thrust for periods up to seven hours, there would be no certainty that the engines, propellers, and certainly skirt material would stand up to the real thing. The heat would be intense and the air full of fine dust particles, for the North African winds were expected to be strong and fairly permanent; forerunners of the spring dust storms.

31

But the colonel seemed suitably impressed by its obvious potentials and left us and Lady B. with the ultimatum that he would give B.P. the go-ahead if a number of modifications were implemented during the next six months: these he would send to Hoverair shortly.

A shapely brunette with a faintly sensual limp led me along the musty corridors of the Egyptian Embassy. The great man had agreed to see me as soon as Mustapha Hamdi had told him our intention to demonstrate the hovercraft in Cairo. All now moved with speed. 'Why had we not earlier said this was our purpose?' The Ambassador saw no reason why we should not take our machines through his country and he would write at once to fix both the necessary permissions and the demonstration in Cairo. This was cheering stuff and a similar change of face was evident with the Sudanese. Their Ambassador, Sir Khatim el Khalifa, was a charming man, and looking more English than the English (not that this added to his charm) was off to Ascot Races immaculate in his turf garb. He had been Prime Minister of the Sudan in 1964 and had steered the country through a period when politics were fraught with interference from every side and no leader had emerged with sufficient foresight and firmness to hold the government together for any length of time. Sir Khatim came to power after the Sudanese October Revolution when the unpopular Military Government was ousted. Many have since accused him of being responsible for the first 'purges' of the South, but there is no proof of this and Sir Khatim is a mild man with a great sense of patriotism, which includes both North and South. He was most enthusiastic and felt that hovercraft could be put to many invaluable purposes in the Sudan. He agreed to write to his superiors in Khartoum and obtain through them the many documents we would need, including letters of permission from the governors of the four southern provinces through which we would pass.

The Kenyans said we were welcome to travel in whatever form of transport we chose; hovercraft were nothing new to them and were treated like motor-boats. Mention of the machines had an adverse effect with the Ugandans who had hitherto raised no objection to our plans. Now reams of letters flowed from their

The Nubian drum dancers
– all male unfortunately –
entertain us by the shores of
the lake.

Mike Broome, the expedition
photographer, badly burnt at
Wadi Halfa when a petrol
cooker exploded.

An awkward moment unloading Baker from the Wadi Halfa cattle barge.

Bilharzia is an ever-present menace in the shallows by the banks. Servicing on Baker's drive engine.

various departments—special import duties would have to be paid and 'flying space cleared'. Not for many months did I discover that the hovercraft had been taken to mean a new and different type of helicopter.

Word had meanwhile got about of our intentions, and a number of letters arrived from would-be explorers, keen to join the wagon. One of these was Jeremy McKenzie, the captain of the British Army Cross-Country Ski Team, who had recently returned from a year in the Borneo jungles where he had formed his own little army from Murrit tribesmen. He was on loan to the Foreign Office at the time and was one of the very few people with the undoubted distinction of being able to speak Murrit. Having done his bit against the Indonesian guerillas, he sadly left the little Murrits and was now keen to visit other climes.

Hoverair had agreed to send an expert driver/mechanic from their trials stables; so with Nick Holder, Peter Loyd and the photographer whom I hoped to get hold of, we would be six— the optimum number. The groundwork now appeared to be behind us, and I settled down to some Arabic with a week of the course to go before the exams. We had three instructors; an Adeni, a Palestinian and a Jordanian. In this manner, the accent of any officer to pass through the Beaconsfield course is so hybrid that even the purest of Arabic speakers is mystified by its origin. The Palestinian had no sense of humour, the Adeni consumed daily quantities of Teacher's whisky and was alternately too dozy to instruct or too belligerent. In one of the latter moods he attacked the Palestinian and provided us with the most entertaining and instructive Arabic lesson of the course. The Education Corps Captain appeared in mid-battle and separated them bleeding profusely from deep scratches. The result was a week of unbroken Jordanian during which the basics of pronunciation were at last give a chance to settle unchallenged by a host of alternative sounds.

I failed the course though the other eight all passed. Some of them were quite definitely thicker than I, so I blamed the Nile preparations. The Journey was on its feet anyway; and, failure or not, I left with the others for Muscat a fortnight later.

# CHAPTER 2

∞

## *Problems Galore*

We arrived at Bahrein as it sweltered at its humid worst with no sea-breeze to wipe away one's sweat. A VC-10 appeared to have been especially laid on for us since there were only five other passengers: we therefore made full use of the first class compartment and the undivided attentions of three hostesses. Climbing from its air-conditioned comfort into the breath-stopping heat of the tarmac, I had unpleasant thoughts of what the even hotter lands of Oman would be like.

A turbanned driver drove us to the Speedbird Hotel, for the B.O.A.C. personnel had instructions for our despatch to Muscat on the morrow. A B.O.A.C. strike baffled this programme and marooned us in Bahrein for a further eight days where we swam, sailed and dined as lavishly as was possible with an eye to the fact that the Sultan was presumably footing the bill. It also meant that we would arrive in Muscat a fairly respectable colour; if not the deep ochre of the accomplished desert warrior, at least not the sickly off-white of Beaconsfield.

The day before leaving Bahrein I heard that the major in my regiment whose letters had been the cause of my decision to join the Sultan's Army was now in Bahrein Forces Hospital on his way to England and expert surgery. Lurid stories were being told of his lone battle with a group of Dhofari rebels and the long hours spent getting back to his base and medical treatment. The facts turned out to be slightly less desperate than the initial rumours, but certainly he had had part of his shoulder and chest shot away and had been stretcher-borne for twenty-

34

four hours before reaching an air base. The Sultan was apparently 'anti-helicopter' and medical evacuation was about as fast as in the days of the Crimean campaign. Food for thought as we climbed aboard the Gulfline Fokker bound for Muscat.

The Fokker stopped at as many Trucial States as could be fitted into the timetable and the comparatively short distance from Bahrein to Muscat took us at least half as long to cover as the London-Bahrein run. Each of the States, most of whom had some reason—whether actual or imaginary—for a boom of 'prosperity', was in the process of keeping up with the Ali Jones's by erecting modernistic, and for the most part purposeless, structures around their airfields. In fact none of the Trucial airports could hope to compete with the ultimate monstrosity of the neighbouring Dohar-drome. At Dubai we watched a company of Trucial Oman Scouts, complete with band, welcome the sheiks of the other states as they arrived for yet another 'federation pow-wow'. These meetings had been taking place with regular zeal and resulting always in complete failure to agree over any of the more tangible points at issue. Bahrein and Qatar were possibly the worst offenders but the sheiks of Dubai and Abu Dhabi were, and are, jealous of one another, and since an alliance will be the only hope for their personal survival if the British leave the Gulf in 1971, their pride will probably be their downfall.

The pilot was unable to say quite when we passed over Omani territory, but we had been flying over vast areas of arid mountain range for some time when the bluest of bright blue seas appeared beneath: the Gulf of Oman. Hugging the sandy coastline and following it to the south-east, the Fokker turned inland and began the descent over oil-tankers, storage tanks, and the neat little bungalows of the oilmen's families. A brief glimpse of the fabled city of Muscat, and the machine descended alarmingly between two mountains to land heavily at the single strip of Bayt-al Falaj, which serves as both the Muscat air terminal and the Headquarters of the Sultan's Armed Forces.

The Sultan himself, Said bin Taimur, was the third ruler of the Al bu Said dynasty; a shrewd and capable man who did all that he could for his country but—unlike his weaker-minded neighbouring potentates—he kept progress within the limits of his country's budget. Oil had only recently been found in the Oman, and before the oil revenues began pouring in, the Sultan had to rely almost entirely on customs duties and a paltry annual grant from Britain. With oil, he was in a more powerful position to improve his country's lot and encourage internal industries along with the health and educational services. But first he had to strengthen his position militarily, for if the British forces were to be withdrawn from the Persian Gulf territories, he would face dangers from both north and south, and possibly from revolutionary extremists within the country. Realising this, he had formed a highly-trained and well-disciplined force consisting of three infantry regiments with limited artillery support, a navy of one arab dhow—soon to be augmented with some gunboats—and an airforce which has just received nine Jet Provost Strikemasters and will acquire four helicopters during 1970. All the officers are British or Pakistani—with one or two notable colonial exceptions—some on secondment from their parent units, and some mercenaries. The soldiers are Omani volunteers or Baluchi mercenaries from the north of West Pakistan.

I was to take over the Reconnaissance Platoon of the Muscat Regiment, which had recently undergone conversion from being mounted on thirty camels to five Land-Rovers: a conversion which the drivers were inclined to forget from time to time, to the detriment of the vehicles' suspensions. The Platoon's patrol area covered the entire region south of the 9,000 foot Al Hajir mountain range, stretching west into the Empty Quarter and south into the Sharqeeya and Wahiba Sands.

The next few months passed quickly, for the work was fascinating and new, but letters kept arriving from Britain confirming my suspicions that all was far from ready for the fast approaching Nile journey: Jeremy McKenzie could not after all join us, for a couple of very good reasons. It would, so his commanding officer had just assured him, put paid to his last hopes of becoming a major, and this would benefit neither his regiment nor himself. He had also met a stunningly attractive blonde in Berlin whom he wanted to marry, and whereas the

Nile was unlikely to vanish overnight, the same could not be said with any degree of certainty of his intended bride. Companies, including B.P., were having doubts about their support and the loan of their equipment; doubts which increased with the deterioration of the situation in Egypt and the Sudan. I realised that, unless the morale of the various supporters could be boosted and their doubts waived, the whole enterprise was in danger of grinding to an inglorious halt.

A close relative of mine died that September and I received three weeks compassionate leave to Britain to attend the funeral. After the sad occasion was over, I visited Britannic House, London home of British Petroleum, where a decision had been made, mainly for political reasons, to extend no aid to our fuelling programme other than recommendations to various connections of theirs in Egypt and the Sudan. Having requested, and expected, aid in the region of two thousand pounds and transporting facilities in inaccessible areas, this was disappointing. However, the firm's chairman was a very reasonable man whom I had met earlier. He responded to my letter of appeal to the tune of a few hundred pounds, and his sales manager wrote to Misr Petroleum, Shell Sudan and East African Shell so that we received an account at the various petrol stations along the entire route. It would simply be a question of actually finding the right garages, which with an up-to-date Michelin guide and A.A. route plans should not prove too difficult.

All the embassies had by now acknowledged our intended schedule and documents of authority began to trickle in ... except from the Ugandans. I went to visit them at their Trafalgar Square office in the midst of some violent public demonstration over the rights of someone or other. The entire staff, including the High Commissioner, were at their windows fascinated at the spectacle of Britain's younger generation passionately engaged in the with-it craze of demonstrating against all and sundry. I found a Mrs. Kelly in the Visa Section struggling manfully amidst a sea of multi-coloured forms, all of which appeared to be entirely uncategorised. I told her of our urgent need for permits and without further ado she produced six stamped and signed visa forms with the Uganda Embassy seal together with a carefully worded form releasing our party from paying duties on equipment and vehicles at the Ugandan border; this she also signed with a flourish and stamped with the same seal.

I had still failed to find a photographer, and this was necessary if we were to make any revenue from the journey. The editor of the *Weekend Telegraph* had shown some interest and I discussed sponsorship with him on several occasions. Unfortunately his syndication board decided that we were asking too much and were anyway behind the times since an S.R.N.4 hovercraft had recently navigated most of the Amazon and Orinoco rivers under the sponsorship of the *Geographical Magazine* and the B.B.C. However, I was put in touch with an up-and-coming film maker who favoured travel features and was also director of a large film-distributing company. He had the excellent name of Malcolm Fancey and was immediately enthusiastic, having but recently returned from a crocodile shooting safari in East Africa, his film of which had been a roaring success. Not until I sent him details of the various visas and injections to be obtained did his zeal begin to wane and his final reason for opting out, after much beating about the bush, was that he had misunderstood the source of revenue for the necessary film equipment; he had thought B.P. were providing some £7,000 specifically for film kit. Where this misunderstanding arose I failed to find out, but we heard no more from Mr. Fancey.

A friend of mine in Muscat had a sister—Dany Brooke, who worked for the *Daily Mail*, producing a sort of daily gossip-column. She responded magnificently to a letter from her brother and, during the final two weeks before we left, found a still photographer and freelance ciné-photographer who agreed to join us and provide their own equipment.

The route and schedule which we envisaged was based on the hydrology of the Nile. The flow of the main Nile at the peak of the flood season (late August and early September) is usually some sixteen times that of the lowest period around mid-April; but more startling is the fact that well over half the volume of water for the year flows down in only ten weeks between July and September: at this period, and to a lesser degree for two months either side of it, the tracks running south in the area of the river are completely submerged and road travel anywhere out of the question. December to March is the best time to ascend the river and by reaching our starting point of Cairo in late February we should narrowly miss the sand-storms in Egypt and Nubia as well as the floods of the Sudan and Uganda. Providing the rains did not come early, the tracks of Southern Sudan should all be more or less passable to Land-Rovers, though we could find no-one who had driven in the area during the last fifteen years.

I was promised R.A.F. transport from Nairobi back to Britain for the two Hoverhawks and two Land-Rovers as well as personnel, but planes to Cairo or anywhere else in Egypt did not exist, nor could I get permission to use a naval boat from Cyprus or even a troop plane to El Adem. Any of these things might have been possible given full Army backing.

Since I was in England on compassionate leave, I took the opportunity to drive down to Strategic Command in Wiltshire to see if a request in person would make any difference. A major in the Greys—my own regiment—was on the staff there at the time and was being as helpful as he could. Whilst I was having lunch I discovered that the man wielding ultimate power over the transport question had been one of the Rhine Army brigadiers I had served under in the not so distant past. This was possibly unfortunate since an incident had occurred which ended in his office with a severe reprimand for the parties involved—particularly for me.

I had organised a large exercise for sixty canoeists and 'trekkers' of the Greys which was to take place in and around the Kiel Canal at its eastern end. The area of my training camp was some two hours drive to the north of the canal on the Schleie River above Eckernfjorde and our training rights did not extend beyond the immediate area of the river. However with only two officers to run the exercise (a third was discounted as an obstacle rather than an aid), the Kiel Canal was a far more suitable area in every way, for both canoeists and land groups could be channelled through a series of easily controlled check-points. By midnight the exercise was going well; no-one had been run down and drowned by the enormous ships which passed every few minutes moving silently but swiftly. Their wash was considerable and, enclosed by the steep walls of the Canal on either side, created a crazy movement in the water which took a long time to subside. The looming hulks were only visible as they approached by the red and green lights—one on each side of the bows. The canoeists were heavily blackened as were their craft but since I and my few fellow 'enemy' were using illuminating flares to discover their whereabouts, they craftily paddled close behind the passing ships, being pulled along by the drag and almost invisible in the large waves of the wash as they passed the check-points.

A particularly large tanker approached and an eager Jock on the bank must have seen the miniature flash of paddles in its wash, for against earlier instructions, he sent up a green light right above the stern of the ship which descended onto her deck and burnt away brightly on a cargo hatch. Little men could be seen running about on the deck; there was much shouting and soon a hose spurted foam which extinguished the flare in a second. But the ship had stopped and now various red lights along the banks began to flash, loudspeakers crackling and producing what sounded very like one of Hitler's wartime broadcasts. "Englander Soldaten" was quite definitely included in the ensuing tirade and I felt it time the exercise ended. I contacted Peter Loyd, the other officer on the exercise, and between us we managed to centralise the various groups and canoes in a couple of hours and, having daubed the vehicle number plates with mud and had all the Jocks remove their grey regimental berets, we left the area as surreptitiously as possible.

Officers in Rhine Army are not meant to drive Army vehicles but the driver of my Land-Rover on the way back that night became drowsy and his driving haphazard. I took over from him and some twenty minutes later was myself woken from slumber by his hand shaking my shoulder . . . I missed the first tree, but bounced off a second into a ditch. Both passengers were only superficially injured and the vehicle's engine still sounded healthy. But the rest of it was an expensive mess to be explained in the dreaded military 'misuse and damage' report.

For many months the Army liaison officers in the Kiel district were unable to trace the perpetrators of what had nearly turned into an international incident; for it transpired that not only had the tanker on which the flare had landed been a Russian one, but its cargo had been of so inflammable a nature that the entire crew were obliged to move about the deck in thick rubber-soled boots to avoid the possibility of causing a spark. I followed the inter-regimental correspondence on the 'Kiel case' with interest as various regiments were busy explaining how it could not possibly have been they, even though they did have troops in the Kiel area. But eventually the finger of justice came to rest on the Greys, and I visited the Brigadier. The same Brigadier it seemed who was now the key to our obtaining free transport to Africa.

Whether or not the above had any effect on the army decision to wash its hands of the Nile journey I did not determine; but by the end of the day the M.O.D. attitude had been made crystal clear. Both the Foreign Office and the Army had come to the conclusion that we would stand in grave danger of arrest and imprisonment. Two of us were serving officers, one of whom worked for the 'royalist cause' in Oman which was the target of much Egyptian propaganda. We would be carrying automatic arms, ammunition, military-type radios and maps, with a large selection of film equipment and telescopic lenses. Our route penetrated the U.A.R.'s most sensitive security areas and crossed all the main Nile bridges. We would pass through the military area of Kom Ombo and close by the Aswan defences: our arrest could be engineered with ease and serve as a convenient morsel of propaganda at a time when large-scale British arms sales to the Israelis were anticipated. When, in November, a group of Israeli specialists in helicopters managed to sabotage the main Nile bridge at Qena, the authorities tightened up internal security throughout the land, in particular in the nine Governorates of the Nile. Any group of foreigners travelling down the Nile-side roads was liable to be searched, not only by the local security and army forces, but by any of the zealous civilian soldiers whose unpractised but eager trigger-fingers were daily primed by government security exhortations. I left Stratco with the feeling that further time spent trying to get anything out of M.O.D. was time wasted, and so arranged an expensive but plausible alternative route to Africa through France and Italy We could catch a steamer to Alexandria from Genoa.

A benevolent motoring association agreed to lend us one of their older diesel Land-Rovers, and I contacted the leader of the recently completed Blue Nile Expedition in order to borrow another. Major John Blashford-Snell is a keen patriot and approved of the idea of British 'sales expeditions'. His own journey had been on a far larger scale; seventy men, air support, base camps and numerous scientists. He had made the acquaintance of the Ethiopian Emperor on earlier expeditions, and had been commissioned by the government to organise a journey of scientific research and also to navigate the unknown gorge where the Blue Nile flows wildly between the Tisisiat Falls and the Shafartak road bridge. He unfortunately had no means of finding me a Land-Rover, but did arrange publicity coverage for the journey, which he said was vital for the furtherance of article and photograph sales at a later stage. He also contacted a philatelic agent who produced some four thousand special envelopes: these were to be stamped, five hundred at a time at each of a series of postal districts along the route, and then returned to London where each set of seven envelopes would fetch two guineas from stamp collectors. This sounded like something for nothing and was therefore highly acceptable, especially since the dealer was prepared to go fifty-fifty on the sales.

The Rover-Company agreed to supply a new Land-Rover with ten per cent discount a week before we left, so all was now in readiness. I decided to check on Hoverair's status quo—for they had been most uncommunicative—and I arranged to meet their sales director, Charles Westmorland, for dinner in London. He appeared at first sight to be rather formidable but I was eager to impress him with the care of our arrangements, the thoroughness of our research, and the great opportunities in the advertising field that the journey would open to Hoverair. A good dinner well-lubricated was the obvious answer to soothing any doubts he might still have. We went to the Quo Vadis off Oxford Street, having first emptied a friend's flat of whisky, and I spent the next two hours listening to an unbroken series of remarkable tales which ranged from the Karamajong, where Charles had prospected for strange metals and jewels, to the Middle East, where he had arranged vast arms deals which ran into many millions of pounds. In the Trucial States Sheik Shakput and he had received, during a visit to a neighbouring sheik a twenty-one-gun cannon salute. He noted that at least three of the white robed 'gunners' with their ancient ram-rod poles had suffered 'pre-ignition' whilst still in the act of ramming and had been propelled from the walls of the fortress together with the other nineteen cannon balls.

By midnight, the hovercraft journey had still not been discussed but I felt Charles would make a suitable report to his board on our plans. He had a train to catch and I agreed to take him to Victoria Station in my mini-van, this being a singularly unimpressive vehicle since a few days previously a milk lorry had removed its bonnet and concertinaed the passenger's door. Shortly before arriving at the station I was overtaking a large postal-van on its curbside when it accelerated and edged in front of me. I also accelerated and though gaining on it, was forced to drive partially on the pavement. A police telephone box loomed ahead, and at the moment of overtaking, contact was made both with the box on the left and the mudguard of the postal van on the right. The next two sets of lights were red but prudence and the postal-van forced me to cross both without waiting. Charles remained silent, but I wondered if he was entertaining visions of his hovercraft slaloming madly between the serried ranks of Nile feluccas and barges, their doom as predictable as my mini's. A letter some weeks later, however, assured me that all was well and two Hoverhawks were being tested for us.

The three weeks of compassionate leave over, I went back to the Oman feeling that God willing, all was ready for the expedition next spring.

On arrival in Muscat I received orders to pack my rifle and field kit and take a plane to Salalah, the capital of Dhofar in the southernmost portion of the Sultan's territories. All the action was taking place here and my colonel felt that I should 'see some fun' for a month, so he had me attached to the Northern

Frontier Regiment which was then stationed in Dhofar. This was a good scheme, for my own unit, the Muscat Regiment, would be taking over duties in Dhofar the following spring and it would be useful to see and appreciate the problems of Dhofar guerilla warfare at first hand before trying to run my own operations in the area.

What is going on in Oman is more than a series of isolated clashes, it is now a minor war. Originally the dissident and rebellious subjects were against their Sultan, Said Bin Taimur, and in 1964 forty of them under their self-appointed leader Salim bin Nuffl, travelled to Saudi Arabia to see King Faizal. At the time King Faizal was feeling antagonistic to the Sultan of Muscat, owing to their mutual dispute over the ownership of the Buraimi oasis; so he decided to aid the rebels.

The rebels were given training and were supplied with arms and mines with which they then returned to Dhofar. Bin Nuffl with his forty followers returned by crossing the Empty Quarter in seven Dodge Power Wagons, a considerable feat which has never been repeated by anyone else. They then blew up some of the Sultan's vehicles and ambushed and killed some soldiers, including two British officers. However the Sultan's Forces managed to capture or destroy all the rebel vehicles and to find most of the arms. The rebels had hidden them in the sand when defeat looked imminent but a Baluchi soldier, who was attending to his ablutions in the time-honoured desert fashion of using stones instead of paper, picked up a stone and noticed the gleaming barrel of a Hotchkiss machine-gun which lay buried in the sand.

Just when the rebels looked like failing completely, China came to their aid and they have never looked back. To-day their uniformed and well-trained strength stands in excess of eight hundred, and they now call themselves the Dhofar Liberation Front, claiming that they are liberating the populace both from the Sultan and from the British imperialists. Men who were once staunch Muslim patriots are now indoctrinated communists with the red booklet of Mao's thoughts in their pocket, his badge on their camouflaged lapel, and a sophisticated machine-gun permanently to hand. They know their country, which is ideal guerilla land, intimately and are daily becoming more numerous and audacious.

The country is of the most unusual to find in this part of the world. Salalah itself has a wonderfully temperate climate and well over a thousand sweet-water springs. Inland from Salalah, across only eight thousand yards of flat and featureless waste, a cliff rises up for over three thousand feet into a clear blue sky, green and luxuriantly covered with rich vegetation. From June to September permanent rainclouds blow up from East Africa to give it a heavy rainfall. In this high ground of Dhofar, wild fig-trees grow as tall as coconut palms and a confusing labyrinth of vertical gorges are covered with dense scrub wherein humming-birds jive, outsize technicolour butterflies twist, and a botanist's paradise of rare succulents and orchids waltz in the monsoon breeze. All this in arid Arabia, a stone's throw from Rub al Khali, the world's most pitiless desert. But in this luxuriant vegetation the rebels manage to thrive.

Beyond the mountains, in the plains to the north, it is again desert. In this upper arid area the Sultan's Forces maintain a small supply garrison from which the Salalah main camp is re-supplied. This means passing vehicles over the high mountain road of Qismim, in the heart of the rebel territory where the guerillas are most active. Indeed the rebels are a great deal happier in the mountain area than the Sultan's mercenaries and plainsmen soldiers, many of whom are scared stiff of mountains even when they are not crawling with unseen hostile machine-gunners.

A couple of days after my arrival and attachment to one of the Northern Frontier Regiment Companies, an urgent message was received from one of the Sultan's garrisons, the fort at the coastal town of Mirbat. Mirbat was one of the ancient frankincense trading centres of the Indian and Ottoman Empires and had been supplying frankincense since as long ago as 2000 B.C. The civilian 'askars' who policed the medieval fort there had just been attacked by some 200 rebels and were running out of ammunition. Our solitary Beaver plane took off at once and parachuted ammunition boxes into and near the fort. We went in a convoy along the coast road but found it had been destroyed where it crosses a deep ravine. A forced march along the beach saw our arrival several hours too late; for the rebels had withdrawn during the night and the only sign of them as we arrived was a dead body, right beneath the walls of the fort, already beginning to fester in the heat, and craters in the walls where the rockets and three inch mortars of the rebels had exploded. We questioned the askars and sent their wounded off in the Beaver. The R.A.F. station in Salalah, where the British aircraft servicing unit consists of some seventy men, was mortared later that night so back we all rushed—since the Sultan had no other available troops in the area. We need not have rushed for the mortaring was extremely inaccurate and was not followed up by a ground attack. But the following day an R.A.F. oil disposal truck was ambushed and its driver's legs mutilated. His companion dragged him free and took cover behind a rock whilst a plume of black smoke rose skywards. We arrived on the scene some fifty minutes later: the lorry was on a gravel plain which is as flat as a pancake and offering not a vestige of cover anywhere, but some six hundred yards to the north, the scrub and small hills, which later rise to steep mountains, start and it was from there that the rebels had sprung their ambush. Captain Bill Prince of the Royal Foresters put the mortars into position a small distance behind the burning lorry and I took two platoons forward with the intention of locating the earlier positions of the rebels and inspecting the empty cases to identify their weapons. To do this meant sweeping in a semi-circle around the truck and some five hundred yards from it. We advanced to within three hundred yards of the scrub without finding any signs and I then tried to wheel the platoons to the right in order to achieve the semi-circular sweep. I shouted various words of command in Beaconsfield Arabic and even in Baluch—to no effect: they all kept heading north for the scrub. I gesticulated wildly and explicitly but to no avail. When only two hundred yards from the beginning of the scrub, a hail of lead issued from its depths and the platoons fell to the ground, more out of instinct than reason, for the only cover for miles was the scrub to our front. Although no-one could see a rebel, our curtain of answering fire of a wildly inaccurate nature gave us Dutch courage. An advance over the plain was obviously out of the question since we were neither Japanese nor was this the First World War, but there was a staff sergeant who had suicidal inclinations and leapt to his feet with cries of 'Advance'. I felt that honour required my own personage to be at least as close to the opposition as this madman (who did not respond to my cautionary shouts) so, bound by bound, we were becoming larger and larger targets to the invisible foe. Fortunately the staff sergeant was laid low with a bullet through the fleshy part of his thigh, and everyone seemed relieved as we became static again. The old Piston Provost of the Sultan's Air Force then arrived and placed some well aimed air bursts and rockets which eventually forced the rebels to withdraw to their mountain strongholds.

Such fun and games are bearable in small quantities and it was with a very light heart that I left for England and the Nile in early February 1969.

The Sultan's Defence Department, who run such affairs as his officers' leave, had been strongly against my getting any extra leave for the expedition, since the British Army term 'adventure training', which is an excellent cover for a multitude of extraneous activities, is unknown to the Sultanate files and certainly no excuse for extra leave. However, during an unusually violent night exercise against another company in the mountains north of Nizwa, seven of my Arabs sustained injuries of one sort or another and my own hand was somehow slightly crushed and one finger joint almost removed. This served as an unanswerable reason for getting away early for proper medical treatment, a chance I seized with all remaining operable fingers if not both hands. So with medical and annual leave, I could expect at least ten weeks free for the Nile wanderings.

# CHAPTER 3

∞

## *Race to Alex*

Berths on an Italian ship were reserved from Genoa to Alexandria on the 20th February so all final arrangements had to be completed in some two weeks. Much of the bits and pieces from various firms had already arrived at the hovercraft factory and I added to the pile of sundries an assortment of stores from the Sultan's Army on temporary loan, such as mosquito nets, machettes and medicinal necessities.

Hoverair were at the time very pleased with a newly acquired test driver who was working for them. He had been assigned to our White Nile expedition as part of his job and, so I heard, had originally showed great enthusiasm for the task. But he had accompanied a Hoverhawk to the Earl's Court Boat Show and there met John Blashford-Snell who was demonstrating his Avon boats from the Blue Nile Expedition. The latter regaled him with stories of fifteen foot crocodiles, of insect and viper ridden swamps, and of bandits who take pot shots at 'anything white which moves'. Failing to differentiate between the various colours of the Nile, our would be driver-mechanic paled at this new presentation of Nileside characteristics and from that moment he must have made up his mind to absent himself as soon as possible from the whole ghastly project.

During the last week of January, the test driver took the newer and better of our two prospective Hawks on a proving run round the Lincolnshire quarry. A new type of skirt had been attached of a much more durable quality than its predecessor, and may well have affected the performance of the craft's steer-

ing responses. Whether or not this was so, the driver performed
an extremely violent turn in high cross-winds and did what till
then had seemed almost impossible; he turned the craft completely over; wrecking much of its fibreglass structure in doing so.

The driver was resuscitated but the craft was a write-off.
After much argument with the management, it was agreed that
we should have a heavier and considerably older machine as a
replacement. I had seen a brand new craft being prepared for
export to Malawi and pleaded for its transfer to the Nile: to no
avail, since it was already long overdue for Malawi and anyway 'far too good to risk' on our journey. So the old craft was
renovated over the next few days and hovered alongside our
other new machine which by then had a new rubber hover-skirt
and was looking most functional. We christened them Baker and
Burton respectively after the explorers whose Nile exploits and
writings had added so much colour and romance to the history
of the river.

Being a great believer in taking too much rather than too little
on any expedition I wandered around the factory equipment
stores, and removed one or two 'bits' from virtually every shelf
in the place; from screws to propeller blades. A journey to
Birmingham and Rover's Personal Export Department produced
a smart new long-wheel-base Land-Rover and, on the way back,
I called in at Velocette's little factory to borrow three spare
250 c.c. engine units for the Hoverhawks. Each craft is powered
by two drive and one lift engine; all of which, by altering a
few screws, are completely interchangeable. They are basically
motor-cycle engines which run on two-stroke petrol oil mix.

Four days before departure, the six of us met at the quarry
pool. Television film sequences were shot of the craft careening
madly over the pond and breaking up the thick ice which lay
over the water. Peter and I could by then handle the craft with a
fair degree of efficiency which seemed just as well since the test
driver was daily growing more surly and unco-operative. I
accompanied him to Peterborough that afternoon where he was
meant to be entertaining a Canadian importer complete with
ten-gallon hat and matching cigar who had come to England
with the main purpose of buying from Hoverair. The red carpet

had been laid out for him in a big way; but I was intrigued when our test driver took him to a small 'factory' in the town where a large number of strange-looking hovercraft of every shape and size were scattered around the premises. We were introduced to the boss and designer of this firm and it transpired that our test driver had not the least intention of continuing with Hoverair for he was already co-operating with this rival firm and indeed spent the next half hour trying to win over the Canadian to make his purchases here instead of with Hoverair.

I confronted Lady Brassey with the news that a new driver-mechanic would have to be found forthwith since there were now precisely twenty-four hours in which to obtain visas and injections for a substitute. She acted with admirable speed: the traitorous test driver left the company at once and, though at first I felt she must be joking, she then summoned Charles—her son—and having told him the evil tidings, explained that there was no course open other than his own presence on the expedition. He showed neither surprise nor dismay, even if he experienced both; his passport went to London within the hour for visa'ing, and he to the local doctor and camping gear out-fitters. He filled a B.O.A.C. travel-bag with tools and fibreglass repair kit, and stowed this with his fishing rod and wellington boots in the Land-Rover. He had decided to fly to Cairo ten days later where he would join us at Shepheards Hotel. Luxury certainly appeared to be his idiom and I hoped he realised that the expedition was not likely to be a protracted riverside pub-crawl.

Mintech produced a list of questions which they wanted answered during the journey ranging from 'the reaction of other river users' to the problems of transportation on land'. Our friendly motoring association had declared their Land-Rover ready for collection. Peter Loyd drove it down from its patrol-station but had only reached London when the diesel engine gave up the ghost in an abrupt but decisive fashion. This—so late in the day—was something of an emergency, but the motoring association were quick to respond to Peter's telephone call and he eventually produced it at the hovercraft factory the morning before we left. It was promptly crammed with photographic equipment of every description whilst its tow-bar and rear wiring were speedily adapted to the corresponding parts on the two-wheel trailer which also arrived that day from Cornwall. A second trailer had come from somewhere up north, the suspension of which looked suitable for a baby's pram but not much else.

We worked late into the night of the 14th and the firm's mechanics chose to desert their wives and dinner to see us off to as fine a start as possible. All was ready when we drew away from the works at midday on the 15th. The gleaming signboards on each Land-Rover proclaimed that we were 'THE WHITE NILE HOVERCRAFT EXPEDITION', and the local Crowlanders turned out in strength to see us off. The trailers and their awkward loads were fifteen feet long and nine feet broad. This meant a width of some eighteen inches beyond that of the Land-Rovers and it took some time to get used to this unseen bulk, especially when the winds were high or the roads slippery.

It was good to be on the way after so much preparation, and with a brief-case beside me full of papers with stamps and official signatures from some seven different countries; with the two Land-Rovers batting along with their strange looking loads, I really felt that not much had been left to chance.


The road from London to Dover was snow-bound and icy; the Land-Rovers colder than charity. South of the Dartford Tunnel a blizzard obscured the road and lorries appearing from the gloomy murk would come perilously close to our wide loads. We spent the night at Old Park Barracks in Dover, leaving the craft on the parade ground which was covered by some six inches of snow. Army grease was smeared over the exposed engines of the Hawks and anti-freeze added to the radiators; strange precautions for a journey up the tropical Nile, but the weather front which preceded us for the next nine hundred miles through France and Italy to Genoa, was snow and driving sleet.

The Townsend Ferry on which we were booked to France was due to leave Dover at eleven o'clock. At ten we were answering the questions of large numbers of reporters, by ten thirty we had persuaded the Townsend people that since the drivers of both Land-Rovers were militarily employed the whole party should be allowed on board at vastly reduced prices; by five minutes to eleven we were searching frantically amongst the piles of papers in my brief-case for an export licence for the hovercraft. One nasty little customs official who must have suffered from an overdose of Teutonic blood in his veins sat stubbornly behind his desk and refused to allow us on board until this particular document was produced. By eleven ten, with every other type of document strewn over his desk; and with at least twelve of us supported by journalists shouting at him, he finally succumbed when we seized his telephone and asked for the Ministry of Technology. The ship's captain, who had been informed of our problem, had had the decency to delay his ship's departure for twenty minutes: I shall always travel Townsend in recognition of his good deed.

We had three days in which to complete the journey to Genoa and with slow speeds imposed upon us by the blizzards, which, if anything, became worse as we went south, we would have to drive twenty hours a day if we were to catch the boat to Africa. A burst tyre in a tunnel section of the Route Nationale caused a half-hour of blaring horns and frustration: the British motorist is so lamblike in his behaviour compared to the French. Near Avignon an oncoming Peugeot spun across the central verge from the far lane and caused Peter Loyd, then driving the front vehicle, to skid to a waltzing halt. His trailer jack-knifed and a large dent appeared in the fibreglass hull of Baker which had almost slid off the back of its trailer.

In Monaco the trailer lights failed on both vehicles for some inexplicable and untraceable reason, and since our speed up the curving passes was minimal, many a racing Porsche and other infernal machine was forced to swerve to avoid hitting us. This was regrettable but garages were all closed and we stopped only to fill up from our own plentiful supply of jerrycans and keep awake with the occasional cup of ersatz French coffee and mammoth pâté sandwich.

The Italian Customs at Ventimiglia were baffled both by the

hovercraft and by the overwhelming amount of documents relating to them. Long queues of tourists in one lane and lorries in another mounted up as all the customs inspectors from the various gates and offices crowded round our triptychs, permits, and around the craft themselves. Much heated discussion ended in the admirable decision that we should carry on unhindered: our Italian flags had evidently been noted and had the right effect. The cameras, arms and radios had been forgotten, and who were we to object.

The Piazza de Ferrari in Genoa is the impressive square—a circular square—where the Adriatic Shipping Line have their main office. It is also the centre of a complex one-way traffic system which makes no allowance for the foolish foreigner who has found his way into the wrong lane. At the slightest provocation, the Latin drivers punch their horns mercilessly and edge in on the poor unfortunate struggling to get to some side road. They do not eye congestions from a distance and if possible avoid them: they rush towards them with joy and enlarge them.

Mike Broome, our still-photographer, drove the long-wheel-base Land-Rover complete with Hawk and trailer into the narrow Via Dante in an attempt at escaping from the Piazza. His vehicle and trailer became jammed across all three lanes at a road junction and a swarm of Fiats closed in from every side. The blinding rain and voluble but ineffective policemen did not help and their attempts at guiding Mike's steering resulted in at least one dented car and one of their number being semi-squashed between the trailer and a wall. With great presence of mind Mike unhitched the trailer and, leaving it so that it obstructed no more than one and a half lanes, drove off in the Land-Rover to find the others, who had disappeared in the mêlée, and a hotel where we might find parking for the 'convoy'. Some two hours later, having found a hotel a dozen 'circular squares' or more away from the Piazza de Ferrari, we returned to the Via Dante, aptly named, and retrieved a forlorn-looking Baker, now almost alone on the road for the rush hour had ended. There was a large official document pinned to the windscreen, but since none of us spoke a word of Italian, there was no way of telling if it was a circular from the Italian communist party or a parking ticket: so it was removed and destroyed.

Later in the evening my brief-case was stolen from the locked cab of the Land-Rover. As we had parked outside the Hotel Londré in the busiest part of the city with street-lights everywhere, this came as quite a shock. Also removed from the cab was my Nikon F camera and the Nikons of Mike Broome and Anthony Brockhouse, the movie man. A pretty haul, for we had not left the vehicle more than five minutes whilst taking other baggage to the hotel. The pride of my possessions and the fruits of my Arabic course—all those precious documents so vital to the journey including letters of introduction to Generals and Provincial Governors in the Southern Sudan—all were gone. Fate burnt its candle from both ends that evening for we heard that our ship *Esperia* was to be delayed some twenty-four hours which at least gave us thinking time in which to work out and if possible allay the worst consequences of the theft. The Genoan Police were politely concerned, scribbled details and gave us forms for later insurance claims. It was obvious that in this notorious Mediterranean den of iniquity, the police had their hands full of problems considerably more urgent than minor thefts.

Anthony, whose Nikon was only incidental to the expedition, since he was after all the movie film-maker and all his ciné kit was safe, was extremely put out by the theft and expressed his doubts that, as the expedition didn't seem to be able to look after its kit in Europe, anything at all would be left by the time we reached Nairobi having traversed the countries of the world's light-fingered experts. I countered this with the observation that recrimination wouldn't help and unless something was done immediately, we would never reach Nairobi anyway.

Mike Broome on the other hand, whose livelihood and whole presence on the journey, depended on his camera equipment, took the theft philosophically and went on a shopping expedition of Genoa's photographic suppliers: he seemed fairly satisfied with a mediocre replacement for his Nikon, but had lost the wide choice of lenses which had been with his camera, and his results were bound to suffer since his scope was now much curtailed.

Telephone calls to the Automobile Association, to the U.A.R. and Sudanese Embassies in London, and to our friend Mrs. Kelly in the Ugandan High Commission brought promise that copies of many of the missing papers would be forwarded to us in Alexandria or Cairo. Through a quirk of fate, all our passports and traveller's cheques had been with their owners and so none stolen: all the same it felt strange leaving Europe without a paper or even driving-licence to our name.

The hovercraft were hoisted—with what we felt to be unnecessary abandon onto an empty area of the *Esperia* but at the far end of the ship from the Land-Rovers. We were naturally enough rather over-touchy about the 'glad eye' of most Italians and all Genoese, and felt that every spectator who fingered our Hawks was coveting either the Velocette engines or our immaculate expedition-signs. God knows why they should have wanted the latter but we weren't in a mood for reasoning and coerced the chief deck-hand into lashing tarpaulin covers over both the craft thereby rendering them relatively thief-proof and also keeping the engines protected from any salty spray which might later come their way.

We left port by dusk, but the pervading wind seemed to follow us with its whiff of Genoese garlic, fish and dustbins, far into the Mediterranean. The seas were high and unpleasantly pitching: our cheap eight-man cabin was at one end of the boat and smelled of deisel. Mike Broome cunningly resisted the attempts of two uncouth Scandinavian hippies, who had scented spare bedspace in our berth, to gain an entry. He cocked my pistol and slowly spun the loaded chambers whilst all the while subjecting the bearded beauties to an evil leer of which Alfred Hitchcock would have been proud. A corpulent woman, dark-skinned but of indeterminable origin woke me up soon after I had at last managed to slumber with the help of three Sealeg tablets; she was slightly hysterical and wearing only a nightdress over her ample self. I cowered back automatically from this vision, but she asked me for a knife. She repeated the request in raised tones and, slightly mesmerised by her appearance and possibly the Sealegs, I handed her one of the expedition knives—a large and lethal thing—which she took and left the room without further explanation. On checking next morning I found that this was not a dream for the knife had indeed gone. I dressed quickly and asked the purser if there had been a suicide on board. A discreet search was instigated when I told him my story and we eventually ran the woman to ground in her cabin where she was squatting on the floor—in the same nightdress—picking stitches from a tweed coat with my knife. So ended my expectations of high-sea drama.

Food on board was bearable but presented in mini-form by waiters who neither spoke nor attempted to understand the simple English request for more which we reiterated at each meal. Soon they became annoyed, after all, the other third-class passengers didn't complain, so why should we? But we had nothing else to do and the sea-breezes produced large appetites, so in the end—by the third and last day—we were receiving reasonably healthy portions. There were two German citizens at our table; one a typically jovial Bavarian named Klaus, the other a Somali who had married and now worked in Germany, named Mohomed Biermaus. They were intending to drive down the east coast of Africa via Port Sudan to Somalia in two ancient Mercedes cars, but when we later met them in Cairo, they had been turned back by a road-block we were shortly to head for, and had to make their way east to Suez.

Three months later Klaus wrote from Germany with the story of their trip... "we have past a very bad time in Suez. Shell-splinters and rockets are flying all ways round our ears... after three days here the fights started. Allways we was sitting in a damned Egyptian cave, and when we leave Suez it was fifty per cent destroit. One day in the harbour I was on the toilette, it comes a rocket near by the ship down, and in the window plenty of shell splinters. It was wonder not one in my body. Troubles, allways troubles with the egyptian peoples. Nobody want to let us in or out. My hopes that you have better times."

The bedlam and boredom of the second-class 'sitting-room' with its babies and sad-faced Jews soon to become Israelis sent us wandering on a tour of inspection. The first-class ballroom, which had as a permanent fixture a musical trio complete with piano, violin and some form of wind instrument, was nearly empty, but on surveying the occupants—all fairly ancient—I noticed a white-haired Englishman with distinguished features that I immediately recognised but took some moments to place. Then I remembered: it was the manager of one of Hereford's largest banks, the name of which it would be unnecessary and unfair to repeat. I ducked instinctively and slipped out of the ballroom, leaving Peter looking very first-class in his ancient tuxedo and chatting to a barman whom he had just treated to a drink.

During February 1966, whilst on a selection course for the 22nd S.A.S. Regiment who were based in Hereford, I was instructed to prepare theoretical plans for removing a fairly large sum of money from one of the Hereford banks. The other officers on the course, though I did not know this, had the same plans to prepare, but for other banks. Fearing that any lack of thoroughness would be condemned as inefficiency, and having only a day in which to complete the plans, I felt there was no time for reconnaissance from a nearby rooftop or posing as an insurance inspector. Such time honoured methods need careful preparation. Having found no brilliant alternative plan, I entered the bank shortly after closing-time and explained to the manager, who was in a hurry to get off to his home, that I was in the locally stationed Army unit having only recently arrived from some years in Germany where I had banked with a Hamburg bank. It was obviously convenient now to open an account with one of the Hereford banks, but one where efficiency and above all security precautions were good. After showing the manager my passport, Army identity card, and both English and German banking deposit-books, we went on a small tour of the building and security arrangements. He was charming and seemed to appreciate my concern about security, but I felt that there were a number of alarm devices which he had not informed me about. However the S.A.S. selection staff were equally unlikely to know of such omissions in my plans, so I thanked the manager for his help and left to make detailed plans which included a scale drawing of the bank-rooms, office, and the security devices which I had been shown.

The planned operation was of course never to take place, but I added theoretical dates and timings for the near future. Since that evening was free, three of us candidates travelled to a nearby town to see a film and dine out; the wine was good and, absent-minded as ever, I left the envelope containing my plans, to which I had been putting the finishing touches, in the restaurant when we left. Being an honest (Italian) British citizen, the restaurateur rushed to his phone on reading the contents of the envelope, and told the police of his find.

The first I knew of this turn of events was the headlines of the national papers on the 14th February. 'Big Bank Raid Mystery' and 'Ministry Enquiry into Bank Raid Scare' were the headings, but by the 16th February this had changed to 'Army's Initiative Upsets Police' and 'Army Raid Starts Police Alert'. Even *The Times* commented that 'it appeared that the services were letting their zeal outrun their discretion in this case'. There had been a twenty-four-hour emergency security operation involving the entire Herefordshire police-force, bank managers had been interviewed, and road-blocks set up all over the county.

Strong representations were also made—as a result of the above chaos—to the bank in question, when the manager eventually told the police of his earlier visitor. His career was not helped by what was considered to be a breach of security on his part. He was not therefore the best man to meet on board a small ship with no other English groups present. I later explained all this to Peter who listened quietly and then told me I was quite wrong: the man wasn't the bank manager at all, he was the new British Ambassador to Cairo and, as such, an important ally to cultivate whilst we had the chance. We suspected that we would probably be his first problem in his new job, for the morning news had said Russia was now arming the Aswan dam with a myriad of new-fangled S.A.M. rockets. Our intention to hover through so delicate an area would no doubt raise a few political questions and eyebrows. Even when I later had tea with the Ambassador and his wife in the impressive Cairo Embassy, in whose gardens we camped, I could not put the thought out of my mind that he was really the bank manager, so great was the likeness between them.

The journey was broken by a few hours at Naples. The Napoleans, as Nick Holder insisted on calling them, were so very different to the Genoese and the gay spirits of the place was immediately apparent; the hubbub of busy shoppers and the amiable police blended well with the lines of multi-coloured washing which hung like festive bunting from every window in every side street. We took a bus to Pompei; Peter suggested that this would be a good way of stimulating our interest in archaeology and things historical, an important aspect of any thorough journey in the lands of the Nile. The petrified bodies of Pompeians caught by an angry Vesuvius and the sensual murals which betray the importance and frankness of carnal pleasures in the era of the disaster—both attractions ensured a full house on the bus from the *Esperia*. After all, not so very many ancient monuments can appeal to both the sadistic and the erotic tastes of their audience. The restaurant situated in the centre of the ancient city can boast of a higher tariff than either of its counterparts in the Eiffel Tower and London's G.P.O. Tower: even the Coca Colas were at a prohibitive price.

The weather improved as we left on the last leg to the Egyptian coast and our spirits were high: the morrow would see us at Alex, twin mouth of Africa's longest and most influential river and gateway to the Dark Continent.

# CHAPTER 4

∞

## *Cities of Confusion*

Without the Thames, London would lose much of its dignity and meaning, England some of her most beautiful scenery; yet even were the river to dry up tomorrow, no national disaster would result. But the Nile is not simply Egypt's life-line, it is her life. No Nile, no Egypt, and since the waters flow from sources in distant lands beyond her control, there can be no way of ensuring that the Nile will always go on flowing. The river brings with it the rich soil of Abyssinia, the Nile silt, which settles wherever the floods go. Every August the flood arrives with this vital nourishment, but where the waters have not been there is no life, for here the sands hold sway and the deserts wait. Sometimes they show impatience and tentacles of sand reach into green fields, smothering life and reminding the Egyptian of his total reliance on the river.

To the north of Cairo, twin rivers with their individual canals and dams fan out forming the famed cotton-growing area known as the Delta. The western branch is the Rosetta Nile, the eastern the Damietta; these have both shrunk since earlier times, but were respectively known as the Canopic and Pelusiac Rivers, the former reaching the sea just east of Alexandria, city of Alexander the Great and once the greatest trading port in the world. During the short reign of the young blond emperor, and later under the Ptolemies and Romans, merchant ships plied into this port from India and China with gems, spice and silk, fine horses from Syria and incense from the Oman. Corn, not cotton was exported, also papyrus and fruits. Greek, Roman and

60

Christian philosophers and scholars, artists and sculptors came to Alexandria as moths to a flame and for years 'the fabulous city' ruled as cultural as well as commercial centre of the world. Some two centuries before Christ, Alexandria was a truly cosmopolitan city: Greeks, Romans, Jews and Egyptians lived and worked in peaceful coexistence, and merchants of every race sought fortunes there.

As the *Esperia* approached the harbour through a motley collection of East European warships, the city's waterfront spread away to either side in the morning haze. Minarets vie with ugly modern structures to clutter the skyline; prayer-towers and cranes mosques and hotels; Allah can distinguish between them, but he must surely wonder from time to time at the appalling taste of his faithful, for he gave them the raw materials—the bluest of seas and skies, the simple lines of the curving natural harbour —and what a mess they have produced in the finished article. Nearer to the western of the two main harbours, we noticed a crumbling 'Beau Geste' fortress which would serve as a perfect film-set for some last Legionnaire drama. This is the Arab 'hisn' of Qait Bay built in the fifteenth century on the site of the famous lighthouse of El Iskanderiya—said to be the incredible height of five hundred and seventy feet—where spiralling ramps led blinded mules to its heights with fuel for the beacon.

MIG fighters made themselves noisily evident overhead as a gaggle of customs and police officials climbed aboard. Our documents problem reared its ugly head at once for no one was being allowed out of the main lounge area, where all had congregated, without numerous forms being first completed and stamped by officials. Since they needed travel *carnets* and vehicle licences in order to fill in the forms, and we had neither; Egypt might still elude us. An official in dark blue uniform with a yellow hatband who was neither police nor customs was idly smoking in an armchair, observing the few women passengers of seduceable age: a miracle in the form of an Egyptian Thomas Cook's agent. He didn't respond to my first greeting, but when I apologetically produced two Egyptian pound notes from a fairly thick wad and asked if he might help me to enter Alex, he

gave a magnificently confidential smile and refused the notes
with an airy wave.

"It is my pleasure to assist you in every possible way, and
must tell you my name is Mohommed: everyone in Alex knows
Mohommed and will help his friends. You are my friend, and we
will have no troubles with my other very good friends the
customs officers. Where are your papers?" This question rather
spoilt what was otherwise a very promising little speech but he
didn't seem unduly perturbed that apart from passport and
travellers' cheques all my papers had been stolen. "Papers make
things easy and quick, but you have Mohommed at your side
so all will be well. You will see."

Mohommed's face did fall slightly when I explained as gently
and gradually as possible that there were four others, two Land-
Rovers, trailers, hovercraft, and an assortment of dutiable items
to excite the eye of any customs officer. However he obviously
had immense confidence in his methods with his very good
friends for he filled in various papers which he had with him
and without trouble obtained the signature of an official at the
desk. Leaving Mike by the hovercraft and Anthony with his
ciné gear and the Land-Rovers—for the crowds of 'porters' and
local seamen who had come aboard looked far more shifty than
even the deck louts of Genoa—we followed our Cook's guardian
angel onto the quay and into the gloomy hall that houses the
various customs officials in their rabbit-warren of glass partitions.

There then followed three hours of the most frustrating red
tape I've experienced in any country. Without Mohommed I am
quite sure we would either have spent the next day in Alex
docks or else back on the *Esperia* steaming on to Tel Aviv. Each
official was busier than the next, and when at last Mohommed
managed to push our documents under the nose of some petty
clerk, and the latter's pen or stamp was poised to deliver the
vital mark, a sheath of dirty bills of lading would arrive, plonked
on top of our papers by some tatty boy no bigger than the desk.
Mohommed had numerous books of reference and addresses in
his pockets, and he kept one pocket devoted entirely to ten-
piastre notes; this enabled him, without checking the value of
the notes in his hand, to place one or two in the ever ready

palms of the customs officials, in so deft a fashion that the whole transaction was complete in a matter of seconds. He had done this on several occasions before I noticed quite what was going on. Neither party made any reference to the handout and the receivers' faces remained expressionless, but I did observe an improvement in the speed with which our papers were dealt with, and thereafter kept a ready stock of ten-piastre notes in one of my pockets.

Clasping the newly acquired customs papers and Egyptian registration plates—light blue to denote our tourist status—we returned to the *Esperia* and soon had their permission to unload the equipment. Leaving a relieved crew of waiters behind us, we left the docks and Mohommed showed us on to the road to the British Consulate. His bill was extortionate and certainly not written into any Cook's fees manuals, however, realising that he had virtually achieved the impossible for us, I paid up happily and he left in high spirits having assured us that Allah would see to our well-being and safe return to America. Since he had seen our British passports, the fact that his fare had not been questioned must have given him a false impression of our wealth and therefore nationality.

We drove straight to the car park of the British Consulate in Alexandria. There were a number of cars and caravans or dormobiles parked there and we talked to some of the occupants. Most had been turned back when attempting to drive south of Luxor on the Aswan road; but some only reached the outskirts of Cairo before being stopped, searched or turned back by a road block manned by military or police officials who ignored their transit visas. We were doubly worried about this as we had no transit visas. However the Consulate was our first poste restante address and on asking inside found that the motoring association had been true to their word for a complete set of new papers and triptychs awaited us.

Also, however, amongst our post was a letter from the British Embassy, Cairo, which had been sent to my home address in England and then forwarded on to Alexandria. It made startling reading bearing in mind that we were already well and truly in Egyptian territory. "... the Ministry of Tourism have reluctantly turned down 'your hovercraft expedition. This must be a great disappointment to you but I am sure you will realise that partly as a result of the Israeli commando raid on Upper Egypt, security restrictions have been increased. Any non-Arab foreigner is to some extent suspect.... Under the present circumstances here, your party might arouse considerable suspicion and the authorities could not guarantee your safety. Mr. Taher of the Ministry said that under normal circumstances your expedition would have been most welcome...." There was nothing we could do about this except in Cairo, so there was no point in getting unduly excited about the letter.

A visit to the maritime station of Alexandria post office took over an hour, for five hundred stamps of the cheapest available issue had to be bought, stuck on to the special expedition envelopes and then stamped with the Post Office stamp. A slip of the metal stamp, and a whole set of seven envelopes would be ruined. The postmaster was baffled and suspicious of our activities, especially when we put the finished envelopes back in their box and failed to post them.

We took with us to Cairo a couple of merry old travellers on their way to Ethiopia. Both were over sixty but were carrying their few belongings in rucksacks. Alan Maundy was a shoe-shop owner from Grimsby, with a face of grizzled leather cracked by the lines of a life of happiness.

"There's nothing in life that's so satisfying as a tramp you know, James" (he never managed to get our names right) "and I've been tramping all my life. My wife used to tramp too, before she died, and many's the wonderful memories we had to talk of in the shop on rainy days. We would spend week-ends on the moors and hills, the year's holiday in Europe or the Scandinavian lands. But I've tramped most of India and Nepal as well and many were the strange sights I saw in those beautiful countries. I was tramping through Turkey last year, taking it slow and easy—for the old body's getting past it—and I stopped on a hill near Istanbul where I met Jane here. We got talking and I saw she had the restless urge same as I do."

It seemed that Jane Simpson, an American spinster, had later visited England and, finding herself near Grimsby, had called

A Manassir tribesman with the weapons of his ancestors.

A tribesman of Paloich inspects his first hovercraft.

"What the hell's that?"

One way of cutting string when you've not got a knife.

in on a delighted Alan. They had decided to join together for a tramp in Ethiopia, if possible to take them all the way from Lake Tana to Addis Ababa. Jane was if anything slightly older than Alan and so frail and dainty to the eye that their project seemed almost a pipe-dream. Anyway they had no transport from Alex so we squeezed them in with us and they stood up well to the long and uncomfortable desert journey to Cairo.

We had planned to take the tarmac road—the Delta route—to the north, but heavy military movement was in progress and we were diverted to the south-east. The narrow desert route was first flanked by salt marsh, and then cut through endless miles of gravel and sand, the northern limits of the Libyan Desert. Sand had in many places blown across and obscured the road surface so that after dusk there was no sign of the motorable route. Only by continuing in as straight a line as possible, for the road must have been of Roman origin, did we come again onto the tarmac.

A trailer tyre was punctured and, in the dark nothing seemed to be in its right place. The jack was nowhere to be found and a new spare wheel for that particular trailer—a different size to the other trailer wheels—turned out to be right at the front of the yellow Land-Rover; the diesel one with all the photographic kit. Patience is a much tried virtue on such journeys, and this was amply demonstrated during the next hour, especially when wheel nuts securing the punctured tyre were found to be jammed solid. I applied brute force to a nut and it broke. This turned out to be because the thread of the nuts was 'continental' and therefore had to be turned in the opposite direction to the normal nut. Someone might have told us; I thought the damned thing had been made in Cornwall. Fortunately Anthony had an inspiration and a makeshift bolt was found to fit the hub perfectly.

We came to the pyramids at Gizeh by midnight. Thirst and dust were forgotten as the dazzling illuminated cones rose quite suddenly into view. The evening's *son et lumière* had ended, but the lights were still on. The moon had come out and was visible as a darting yellow boomerang between racing nimbus clouds: pi-dogs howled from the sands, but the glow of Cairo's

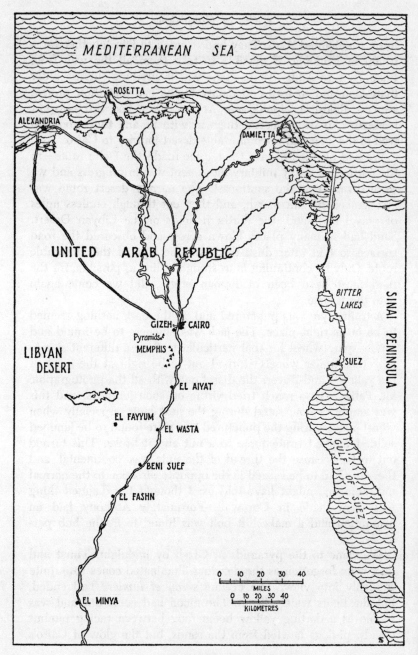

The Lower Nile

lights was already visible to the east. Not far from ancient Memphis, seat of the Nile gods and their priests, the first Muslim invaders in the seventh century built the fortress of El Fostat. As it was built, the planet Mars was in the ascendant, known to the Arabs as El Kahira; the victorious planet. This later became the site of Kahira or Cairo, the new capital, for the first conquering hordes of Islam had brutally sacked Alexandria which would never again rise to even a vestige of its former glory.

Our first glimpse of Cairo, the three pyramids of Gizeh, remains the strongest impression my mind holds of the city and its environs. Pictures of power and uncaring megalomania are conjured up by these impersonal monuments to long-forgotten kings. We left the pyramids and stopped at the Mena House, a long elegant building amidst tall trees and subtly-lit gardens where honeymooners sit and stare at one another, sipping tall expensive drinks; whilst music—Arab and European—issues from boxes in the foliage. The Mena House is now one of Egypt's few really first-class hotels and was also the first in the country. It was built by the Egyptian King Mena as a small palace from which he and his entourage could watch the Nile and get away from the cares of Memphis.

Not wishing to get lost in the suburbs of Cairo or do a repeat performance of our night in Genoa, we phoned the night watchman at the Embassy in Cairo and in half an hour some young officials arrived to guide us to the Embassy compound which they said was the only safe place for our vehicles. They had also arranged accommodation: Peter and I stayed at a nearby club, the others with a young Canadian woman whom we had met on the *Esperia*. Our passengers, the over-sixties, were grateful for the ride but determined to make their own way southward on the following day.

The British Military Attaché, who welcomed us despite the forbidding letter we'd received in Alexandria, understood that since the letter had only reached us after our arrival in the U.A.R., we had come in all faith and hope. He explained that a worse time for such a trip would have been difficult to find, with deep suspicion of all foreigners at its most hysterical, owing to the penetration of Israeli saboteur groups far behind the front lines. One of the prevalent theories as to the methods of these commandos was that they disguised themselves as tourists and moved mainly by night. The Government had also announced—the very morning we arrived in Alexandria—that a state of emergency would be observed throughout the country, which meant the arming of the citizen forces and the sandbagging of all buildings. Tape was stuck to the window-panes, blackout cloth in use and Civil Defence lectures provided for all and sundry in most towns. But we felt that it would take a few bombs, not just radio lectures, before Cairo dwellers took such things as a blackout seriously. We had seen the blaze of Cairo's nightlife from at least five miles west of its suburbs as we approached from Alexandria.

At all the barrages, dams, bridges, and even minor irrigation gates, standing patrols watched for any sign of saboteurs. It seemed that they had some idea of Cockleshell Hero-type raids since sandbagged positions overlooking the river at strategic points were permanently manned although some way from the front line. The sudden sight of a hovercraft, never seen before on Egyptian soil or water, might well have provoked immediate action from the guards. They might have thought it was some new Israeli infernal machine come to destroy the United Arab Republic. What quicker way of obtaining everlasting glory than to destroy this monstrous new machine whilst it was a sitting duck on the water's edge?

Hovering on any part of the Nile in Egypt was therefore quite out of the question, and since there were also some ninety road-blocks between Cairo and Aswan, a road journey was a pretty doubtful alternative; it was also the only alternative. The Military Attaché knew of no-one who had recently been allowed down the road, and said several people had been turned back, as in the case of our German friends, from a road barrier reported to be only some five miles south of Cairo. However, he had friends in the Ministry of Tourism both in Cairo and Luxor and said he would do his best for us. We decided to attempt the 'breakout' the next day, and spent the afternoon making arrangements to fit in with the altered programme, now that hovering was no longer permissible in the Egyptian sector of

## Cities of Confusion

the Nile or anywhere their side of the Sudan border. Since we were strictly 'The White Nile Hovercraft Expedition', and the White Nile only begins (or ends, strictly speaking) at Khartoum, it made little difference how much hovering we did before reaching the city, apart from prestige value to the hover firm, and having to alter our original plans. A further problem this caused was that we would have to ship the vehicles through Lake Nasser since the roads bordering it had been submerged.

The Sudan Railways' Cairo office was not easy to find but we had been told it was impossible to get tickets elsewhere for the steamer journey we would have to make from Shellal, by Aswan, to Wadi Halfa. A wizened little Turk who spoke excellent English pointed out that since there was only one ancient steamer making the two hundred and eighty mile journey and towing a couple of flat barges, reservations had to be made well in advance. If we required first-class, payment was also in advance, and in the event of our missing the boat, not refundable. A one-sided agreement, but there was no other way to Wadi Halfa. The Turk was startled when he saw my name on my passport. My father's names were exactly the same as my own and the Turk had apparently served with him in Palestine many years back before the war. He gave us coffee and recounted interesting stories of those earlier days. When I later asked for berths for the vehicles and trailers he was explicit.

"The barges towed behind our steamer are not intended to carry cars; one is for passengers, the other for cattle and fruit and its roof for third-class passengers. The entry onto either barge is narrow and fairly low; the decks dotted with steel uprights. Even a single Land-Rover would have difficulty getting on board, and I gather your trailers with their loads are longer and wider than the Land-Rovers. It seems most unlikely that you will manage it, but since there is no other way, I'll give you the reservations which are not redeemable, and wish you the best of luck."

Back at the Embassy compound, I was re-stacking the tool kits in the vehicles when the new Ambassador strolled by inspecting the gardens. I was scruffy and oil-besmeared but he didn't seem to mind and asked me to tea. The inside of the Embassy

69

was even more impressive than the grandiose exterior; ornate and lavish, but everything in the best of taste and immaculately kept. It seemed sad that the Embassy was soon to go elsewhere; doubtless to some neat modern block. Here Baring had sat to ponder the numerous problems of his Egypt—which he ruled just as surely as did the Ptolemies or the Turks, though with a far greater humanity. Here, too, Kitchener, whose personal uniform still lies in the cellars, discussed his campaigns. The whole atmosphere of the place is of bygone splendour, and the Ambassador admitted that he and his wife felt far from homely in their new residence. Tea arrived silently as it had done for centuries by the hand of tall Nubian servants in white djellabias with wide red sashes, who performed their tasks with ritual exactness.

The Ambassador's wife was Spanish and charming; they had been married for twenty-five years and travelled extensively with his diplomatic posts. Cairo was a rest-cure to him after a series of trouble spots, but when I thanked them and was leaving, he warned me to be particularly careful should I hear of any arms deal contemplated by the British with the Israelis. All was peaceful between the two countries at the time but there were rumours of some two hundred and fifty Centurion tanks for sale, and should the British sell these to Israel, Egypt would become most unsafe for us overnight.

Peter and I left the club of the night before which had proved much too expensive, and joined the others at the luxurious flat of a Canadian called Marjorie, in the Nileside suburb of Zamalek. A magnificent meal had been prepared for us with a fridge full of French and Algerian wines. Charles Westmorland had arrived—complete with three-piece London suit and that day's *Financial Times*—so we were now eight in number. Our hostess had ample balconies running along the front of the flat and was delighted that we should all spend the night there.

Marjorie was interesting to listen to and there was little she did not know about Cairo. Whilst all the while stacking plates with her exotic menu she kept us attentive with a succession of tales of the ancient Cairo; I think she had a genuine love for Egypt, but one which derived from what she had read of the country, and her year in Cairo had somewhat disillusioned and saddened her, for these were troubled confusing times and the city had an aroma of suspicion about it difficult to forget or ignore.

We discussed the Egyptian Jews and their present status. To go back a bit—to about 1900 B.C.—the Hebrew Youssuf (Joseph) was the most revered Egyptian statesman and chancellor of the Pharaoh's exchequer. Through his wisdom he saved the country from the greatest famine it had ever experienced, and became the hero of Egypt. But some four hundred years later when his descendant, Moses, was born, the Pharaoh of the moment was worried at the growing strength of these children of Israel. All the eldest sons were to die, but Moses was saved by the Nile. Sheh means waterbed or Nile, Mu child, Musheh, or Moses—child of the Nile. So some of the Hebrews had their birth pangs with Egypt as their cradle, and today's Egyptian Jew is as strongly Egyptian by instinct as the next man. But the worldwide anti-semitic hates and jealousies are present here too and were so long before the recent Israeli troubles started. The Egyptian Jews have always considered themselves a cut above their fellow 'fellahin', merchants, or members of whatever social strata they find themselves in, and this together with their almost inevitably alert money sense has alienated their neighbours here as elsewhere. Only rather more so for poverty in Egypt is very much more the rule than the exception.

This overall poverty is closely connected with a high incidence of drug-taking. Charles had commented that afternoon, after visiting the backstreets of the city, that drugs and hashish smoking in Nargile pipes seemed commonplace.

We all wondered if hundreds of dealers, smugglers and street vendors lived on the proceeds of what seemed to be the most thriving drug-market of all the Mediterranean countries. The price appeared to be so much lower than in Europe and other North African lands; presumably the opium and other forbidden powders could arrive easily in the Delta from West and East Europe as well as the Far East. We gathered that the police were said not to be over-successful in discovering the countless caches, nor were they over-zealous, for the 'stoned' fellah remains hardworking, and after all, what else has he got to enjoy in his simple weary life?

Mike thought that the Russians might bring in drugs in their ships for he had noticed a number of Russians about that afternoon and he had seen Russian cars and jeeps in Alexandria and Cairo.

Marjorie affirmed that there were indeed a great many Russians and had been since the start of building the Aswan dam. The fellahin did not seem to care for the Russians much for they found the communists a surly lot who kept themselves to themselves. The Russians lived on special housing-estates and only came out to shop and sight-see, which they seemed to do in complete silence. To the cheerful Egyptian fellahin who love to greet each other and strangers too with much handshaking and endless blessings, these silent foreigners appear most unfriendly. She did not think the Russians had anything to do with the import of drugs as drug-taking had occurred on a large scale throughout the Delta long before it spread to European cities.

Marjorie was lyrical over Cairo's antiquities which today are unchanged in atmosphere and tradition from what they were a thousand years ago. The ancient mosque-cum-university of Al Azhar, still the centre of all Muslim study where—for all the modern faculties—the Koran is the real basis of law and study. Behind the neat but dirty flats of the workers in old Cairo, lurk the tombs and monuments of the Mameluke potentates, the work of lavish imaginations which could never have envisaged the square and ugly structures which now enclose their exotic walls. Innumerable minarets, domes, and intricate muezzin towers of prayer dot the city and ensure that every district keeps its character in an ever-changing skyline; a whiff of spices and the mysteries of Kubla Khan still waft through Cairo.

Toasts to our Nile venture and to Alan and Jane on their Abyssinian tramp ended a memorable evening and I felt that if all Canadians were anything like Marjorie, they must be the most hospitable people in the world. We bedded down on the balcony overlooking the Nile—for Zamelek is virtually an island—and watched the fire-crackers explode in bursts of colourful sparks from all around. It was the night of the annual feast Bairan al

Adfah when the fasting period ended and all appetites were fully indulged; a night of merriment and later, love. Slightly downstream we could see the island of Rhoda and shifting paths of light revealed the jostling crowds, their gay screams coming to us over the dancing chintz of the river, over the lilting chant of many thousands of Muslim voices praising their Creator who gave them the Nile and therefore life.

We got little sleep that night, for the festivities went on till dawn with no lessening in the intensity of the chanting and drummed accompaniment; the cats and bullfrogs of Zamalek did their best to compete, and the overall cacaphony hindered any attempt at dozing off.

# CHAPTER 5

∞

## *Heart of Egypt*

The road from Cairo lay south into the midday sun. With three of us in the front of each Land-Rover in hard-topped cabins the heat grew uncomfortable. Shirts stayed on, for the last thing we wanted to do was offend the locals, and Muslims dislike any part of even the male body being revealed in public. Five miles from the last of the Cairo suburbs, the Military Attaché left us and with mixed feelings we watched his official Land-Rover disappear. Everything now really depended on our reception at the first road-block and check-point, for once we had got past one we would have some sort of a leg to stand on.

El Aiyat was the first village of any size we came to and the road vanished in a seething mass of curious Arabs, evil-faced fruit vendors, overloaded mules and camels, none of whom seemed to acknowledge the road to be our right of way. On the contrary, their intention seemed to be our retention there for all to see, for not only were we foreigners—and so always good for an enjoyable scrutiny—but what were these remarkable machines behind our cars? "Tayyara abyad" was the cry taken up by a particularly astute youth and passed on from mouth to mouth in the rising din which soon surrounded and swamped us. "White aeroplanes," quite why Baker and Burton had been dubbed as such, seeing that they obviously had no wings, was difficult to work out, but at least they diverted the curiosity from our persons. As gently as possible I edged forward in first gear, smiling fixedly at all and sundry, in the wild hope that the others would follow and that El Eiyat would come to an end as

74

soon as possible. It did, but its inhabitants were persistent in their curiosity and not for some half-hour, when we were well clear of the place, did we shake off the last shrieking youngster and yapping cur.

Nick agreed that a feeling rather like claustrophobia was experienced whenever we found ourselves in these alarming crowds. Were we to stay put for an hour or more, as when changing a tyre and resting overheated engines, they wouldn't lose interest and disperse; far from it—everyone would rush off to find their friends. Workers from the fields and merchants from their dingy offices would swell the throng, and since it got worse from village to village, we began to suspect they were telephoning ahead to friends to line the route and see the 'extraordinary white aeroplanes'. Mostly it was quite friendly curiosity and interest, but once or twice a vicious face pressed close to the windows and shouted angry words; the occasional hard thump on the sides of the vehicle as of a fist or foot. We had a ready collection of piastre coins, virtually valueless, to give as 'baksheesh' on the inevitable demands, and cigarettes to mollify those whose mules or possessions had been pushed out of the way by our slowly advancing bumpers. Our patience and schedule suffered badly that first morning.

The trailers could so easily have crushed someone, particularly the children who were swept ahead of the mass of onlookers as the sharp corners of the trailers were almost on a level with the heads of the younger ones. The Military Attaché had warned us that even a dog or chicken run over would almost certainly cause a rumpus with the locals even if the owner of the creature wasn't present. A child run over in error in one of these crowds would make life very unpleasant indeed, as we were later, and in different circumstances, to find out.

Even by Arab standards the streets were crowded for, being Bairan al Adfah, everything was happening, and to stay inside meant to miss the fun.

Shortly before we entered the town of El Wasta, a crude barrier pole across the road halted us. There was a small hut as for a bus stop shelter on the control side of the barrier and from this now issued an impressive looking policeman followed by a number of swarthy henchmen in grey trousers and white shirts. The former saluted us and looked us over with open curiosity. He looked at our vehicle documents and letter from the Embassy. He kept this last and disappeared into the hut, presumably to telephone. When he eventually came out and spoke to us, his English was very reasonable.

"You are the helicopter trade party from England going to the foot of Africa, yes?" We nodded our immediate assent. "I have been only today informed of your movement through my district. You understand that you come at a very bad time and normally my orders must be to send you back. However it seems the Minister of Tourism is decided that you must come through and that I am to provide men to ensure your safety, for our people are rightly suspicious of all strangers in this troubled time. This is the Governorate of Beni Suef and we will see you through to the El Minya Governorate by this evening."

Judging by our rate of progress to date, it seemed unlikely to me that we would reach El Minya much before midnight, but the little policeman used the phone again and soon a pair of old vans with klaxon horns and flash-lights mounted on their roofs drew up from a side road. He climbed into the front one, his men separating between the two. We followed him past the road-block and the second van drew up behind Burton, the rear hovercraft. As if to make up for our earlier delays, the police drove alarmingly fast and kept both the klaxon and flashing light permanently on, whether there was an obstacle visible or not. This would have been admirable had the roads been reasonable but the pot-holes were large, deep and dangerous. Should one of the small trailer wheels go into one, there would almost certainly be a puncture and probably buckled suspension too. So we slowed down to a speed which made pot-hole navigation possible and ignored the frustrated signs of the white-shirted goons who stared at us from the rear windows of the leading van.

The cavalcade proceeded with no sign of the earlier crowded roads; even the donkey carts and swerving cyclists melted away before the lights and siren of our escort. We soon came to Beni Suef town, bustling and relatively modern, with a number of impressive new buildings and a business-like community with a high percentage of suits instead of the usual djellabia robes. To our surprise we were escorted to the town hall for soft drinks and Turkish coffee with the Deputy-Governor of the Beni Suef Governorate. We all sat around a man-size portrait of Nasser with a dusty Egyptian flag above it. The drinks were good, but our attempts at conversation with the deputy-governor and his associates were unsuccessful, though he said, as we shook hands with the entire town council, that although hovering and photography were out of the question at the present time, he was pleased to see us and assured us of a continued escort to see us out of his province. A grinning Nasser watched us as we left the room, but with an escort to clear the way and the possible prospect of civic receptions all the way up the river, we felt things were going well.

The eighty miles to El Minya went quickly for the road is well-graded, but the trailer wheel, the one with the continental threads, came off at speed and the end of the axle slewed a deep gouge in the hot tarmac before Nick swerved to a halt. The wheel ran on into the ever-present canal—most Egyptian roads are built on canal banks—and was fished out again by the equally inevitable local lads. How lovers ever find privacy in the Egyptian countryside beats me, for half-naked urchins seem to grow out of the ground if one stops in even the most desolate spots for more than five minutes or so. Fortunately the axle seemed undamaged, and we replaced the four hub bolts which had sheered through, putting back the same wheel.

Having eaten nothing since leaving Cairo, we drew into a side road with a freshly-painted hotel on the corner. A dormobile was parked outside complete with G.B. sign. We joined a Scottish teacher and his wife who were having tea in the roof restaurant. They had been on their way to Aswan where the teacher, who was obviously something of an archaeologist had been intending to visit the Elephantine Island and make some notes on the nileometer (a platform of sloping steps used by the ancient Egyptians and later inhabitants to measure the annual flood levels). They were well provided with permits and visas and had got as far as Luxor before being turned back, in spite of their official papers, at a recently erected road-block just south of the town. We took our time over tea, accompanied by giant wads of goat's cheese sandwiches, and found the Scotsman to be very knowledgeable on Egypt and its fascinating past. We got him talking about the river, his pet subject.

The Arabs, he said, have done little to alter the river and its ways. All that is characteristic of the Nile—the water-wheels, the boats, the monuments that have made its banks so famous— all were here long before the Arab invaders. The Egyptians fashioned them and they have changed little over the centuries. We hadn't seen many water-wheels yet, but after Minya, when the road and river touch from time to time, we should get a close look at some. In early times the desert herdsmen, who first settled by the river, filled their skins and gourds and carried them up the bank on their backs, but once they started cultivating little plots, more water was needed, and about 7000 B.C., the 'shaduf' first appeared on the scene in much the same form as it is today. During the low water months it can be twenty or more feet from the river to the level of the irrigation channels in the fields. Most shaduf consist of two or three palm-wood poles each six feet higher up the bank than its predecessor. Each pole has a skin bucket or tin container for scooping water on one end and a balancing weight of dried mud attached to the other; an upright, also of palm-wood, under the centre of the pole serves as a fulcrum. The man operating the bottom pole lifts water to a pool dug into the bank some four feet above him, the second and third operators repeating the performance until the water flows down the irrigation channels and finds its way to every thirsty plant.

Of course the shaduf is a poor second best to the water-wheel and not really a great labour saver. The 'sakiyeh' is the fellah's best friend for it fetches water without need of his well-muscled back. It's probably a Greek gimmick since there's no sign of it in the tomb murals; and yet they were a going concern long before the Arabs arrived. A camel or oxen is strapped to a horizontal wheel which drives a vertical one with clay gourds or old cooking-fat tins fixed to its rotating outer rim. The owner of a sakiyeh is usually fairly well-off; for land and water means money here more than anywhere else. Often tin cans are fixed to the

revolving wheel and the clattering music caused by their movement assures the overseer in the shades of his nearby house that
the water is flowing; that the little boy who whips the ox when
it idles has not himself dozed off.

Gordon and Kitchener also found the water-wheels useful for
when their steamers ran short of fuel, the palm-wood of the
sakiyehs burnt well in their boilers in a land where wood was as
costly as gold.

Our police escort who had sat themselves down at the next-
door table were on their third round of the locally bottled
beverage, an unbelievable cross between sherry and whisky. They
seemed happy and in no hurry to push on.

"Where will we get a chance to photograph the old steamers?
I heard they're still active on the Nile, unchanged since the
days of the Mahdi." Mike Broome's mind was never very far
from photography.

The Scottish teacher informed us that the only steamers left
in Egypt from those early days were doing the Aswan to Wadi
Halfa run, so we would have plenty of time to photograph them
if we managed to get that far. There used to be a hydrofoil
doing the tourist run to Abu Simbel, but it had been withdrawn,
and there wasn't much on the river now other than the occasional
small dhow, myriads of feluccas, and the odd dahabeeya. The
dahabeeyas were used by the proud Victorian English for Nile
tours, floating house-parties and romantic honeymoons which
often turned sour through the unaccustomed heat. Under gently
flapping sails, these floating houseboats fashioned from the
hardest of local woods, the sunut tree, and crewed by Nubians in
the smartest but most inappropriate uniforms, progressed
majestically upriver. When the breeze died down the crew would
literally pull the boats along by harnessing themselves to long
tow-lines and plodding along the hot and dusty bank: I always
think of the slaves who pulled the vast chunks of granite from
the Nubian desert to Memphis when I see a dahabeeya, and
picture our grandparents cruising in style with their fans fluttering as the tow-lines creaked.

Some of the feluccas depend on haulage for a living, like the
Rhine barges, but many are used for local fishing and inter-

village taxi services. The Nile perch which grow to phenomenal sizes in the upper Ugandan reaches of the river are smaller but just as delicious in Egypt. Moon-fish, which have a supernatural aura about them and are even said to be responsible for the drowning of sinners who dare to swim in the river, can sometimes be seen streaking crazily through the water with their fiercely spiked backs glistening; they fill themselves up with air in some strange way from time to time and, when they feel it's time to deflate, issue a weird noise rather like a rampant whale. This doesn't do them any good when the fishing fellah lays his net, for moon-fish is a tasty addition to any menu. There is also an electrical fish, the malepterurus, which can stun a swimmer by touching him and though it looks like an eel or snake, has small legs and lungs which it could presumably use if it wanted to, though it's never been seen on land.

The Nile crocodiles and hippopotami were unsettled with the Aswan dam springing up like the Berlin Wall. They dislike being disturbed, and the ever-growing river traffic puts them off. There are none now downstream of the High Dam, but there was certainly a time when both animals abounded there and as far north as the Delta. Sobek, one of the most influential Egyptian gods had the head of a crocodile, and the Faium oasis — the largest in the country — was known as Crocodilopolis in the days of the Ptolomies. Hippo, too, had their day and can be seen in the murals of tombs north of Memphis. A king of the wild Hyksos invaders once sent messengers to a vassal prince in Thebes ordering him to destroy all the hippos in his area, for their nocturnal roaring was disturbing his sleep. The Pharaohs used to hunt crocodiles and hippos with long lances from narrow hunting-barques. Hippo hunting must have been cruel and senseless rather like Spanish bullfighting, and with even less risk to the hunters.

Cruelty was never a characteristic of the Egyptian peasant folk, the fellahin, who even now form the majority of the population. Most of them are direct and undiluted descendants of the ancient Egyptian with no trace of Arab blood and sadism in their veins. In the thousand-odd years since they've been here the Arabs have, with the help of English efforts at emanci-

Trouble with suspension south of Malakal.

The retreat from Moscow.

Midday halt near the Sobat River.

Burton passes a houseboat near Malakal — once a proud river-steamer
in the latter days of the Raj.

pation, instilled a certain feeling of pride and self-reliance into the fellahin which they certainly never had under their foreign rulers nor their native kings, the early Pharaohs. A small portion of the population only are truly Arab by blood; strange when one considers that this is the country now spearheading the cause for Arab unity and power.

Our escort were showing signs of impatience so we left the Scots couple and carried on to El Minya, arriving well before dusk. The escort vans went back to Beni Suef, klaxons still jangling, and we were left in the walled compound of the government school with a police detachment presumably to keep us unmolested by light-fingered fellahin. Charles slept beneath the stone arcades of a dingy outside corridor flanked by half a dozen latrines; surprisingly. the air was clean, probably because the cisterns had long since ceased to function and were out of use. A corpulent policeman, who couldn't possibly have had a change of uniform since it had been issued to him, had detached himself from his fellow gate-guards on smelling our coffee and cigarettes. He had sat watching us until provided with both and then formed a protective devotion to Charles who had been swearing at him profusely for a shameless scavenger and communist lackey. Much to Charles's distress, this devotion found the fat policeman bedded down next door to him, and although he placed a screen of camping equipment between them, the atmosphere was unpleasantly heavy. They were now snoring loudly together in a discordant rasping melody which we recorded on tape and played back, much to Charles's embarrassment, the following morning.

We discovered that night that the Egyptian brand of mosquito bites deep and often, though its approach flight is silent; the resultant itch is brief and can be slept through if the victim is sufficiently exhausted. A harmless insect really, in the light of our later unintentional research into the Sudanese variety.

Shortly after midnight, I left the Land-Rover in which I was bedded down intending to visit the scrub at the edge of the compound, there being no workable lavatories to hand; the gate-guards had long since retired and I could hear their adenoids rattling from the lean-to gate. Great was my alarm then when,

F

shortly after I had settled harmlessly behind a bush, two small but efficient little goons came running across the compound with much cocking of machine-pistols and cries of 'Waqqaf' which means 'stop' in anybody's Arabic. It was quite amusing to watch their expressions; even in the gloom their faces registered their disappointment that I was quite definitely not in the process of scaling the compound wall. They retired scowling with a few unintelligible, but presumably choice rejoinders, and left me to my meditations. It struck me that our elaborate escorts might not be solely to protect us from possible persecution, but to ensure that Egypt's military secrets were kept well away from us and our array of telescopic camera-lenses.

This line of thought was borne out, on reflection, by our experiences of the evening before. Shortly after arriving and parking the vehicles and craft in the compound, we had told the police-officer of our keen desire to see the sights of Minya. This didn't please him, but he was obviously a zealous young man and presumably thought we had full ministerial backing and approval. He took us to the Police Club, a pleasant sort of pavilion with lawns and gardens on the banks of the river, from where we wandered, keeping close to our guide like so many sheep. He showed us the chalk yard where great hulks of locally mined and shaped slabs for building await shipment downstream by felucca barge.

He then suggested that we have a look at the sights of Minya by cab; he paid the cabbies to take us round in two hansoms whilst he followed in a third. There are no taxis in Minya, just old hansom carriages which have immaculately polished brass lanterns and are drawn by fine Arab horses. The horses are led into the river at sunset every evening, where the river runs fast and the Nile killer bugs are least likely to infect them. Here the owners wash them down lovingly with handfuls of wet sand.

We felt like something to eat, so our guide took us to a homely restaurant in a backstreet, where the proprietor was said to speak French and English. He didn't but understood the signs for scrambled egg, bacon, and beer which were luridly but explicitly executed by Charles. There was but one door to the cafe and our police friend remained in his cab parked in front of it, having politely refused an offer to join us.

The restaurateur, noticing we were sweating profusely, suggested we adjourn to his roof restaurant (translation of one hand wiping sweat from his brow whilst his other pointed up to the sky and he smiled expressively). We accepted willingly and were delighted to find some tables and chairs on the roof-top where a cool breeze and panoramic view of the Nile added spice to the lukewarm beer and jaundiced eggs.

Settling back to admire the view, it was difficult not to notice the carefully walled-off goods yard with its lines of loaded trailers. Having spent five years with a tank regiment I found little trouble in classifying the bulky shapes under heavy tar-paulins; there must have been some sixty or seventy of them on three separate lines facing north (since there were terminal buffers at the southern end). Away to the left a large airfield stretched into the distance with neat lines of silver-grey jets by long hangars. Peter, the only pilot amongst us, had no doubt that these were MIGs of some sort, and the airfield probably the Abu Qur Qas drome which was marked on our maps.

If this was some secret military depot it was almost certainly known to the Israelis, even if not to most Egyptians, but the authorities might well be chary of our presence in the area; I felt the restaurateur might suffer official wrath should the police find us on his roof, so we descended rapidly and, smiling blandly at Big Brother who was still immobile in his cab, we returned to our compound.

Luxor was to be our next stop and we hoped to traverse Qena Governorate in a day. Our police guide had said there was nothing much to see in the immediate area of Minya though he advised a visit to Tel el Amarna, a few miles upstream and on the far bank.

Tel el Amarna used to be called Akhnaton, which means 'horizon of the Sun', and was once the fabulous palace of Amenophis IV, a young Pharaoh who inspired and carried out Egypt's first religious revolution. Whilst still a youth he decided that the existing gods were so much rubbish, except for the Sun god Aton whom he considered to be the only true god worthy of his, and therefore his subjects', worship. Being of a thorough nature, young Amenophis changed his own name to Akhnaton, sacked the powerful priests of the other gods, destroyed murals which referred to them, and even moved his palace from Thebes to its present site 300 miles farther north, in order to escape from the atmosphere of the ancient gods that prevailed at the former capital. Of course no sooner had he died than the old gods were restored by his successor and the royal court returned to Thebes.

He was something of an individualist, which is more than can be said of the other Pharaohs who were keen on conforming and usually went out of their way to avoid crossing swords with the priests. Near Tel el Amarna is the Serapeum at Abu Mengal which is anything up to eight miles of subterranean tunnels and burial chambers where thousands of sacrificed baboons and ibises are preserved, mummified in individual coffins. This is the same sort of thing as rich American women indulge in with their pet poodle-dogs; but the baboons and ibises were kept for religious not sentimental reasons, for they were the creatures of the god Thoth.

The gods of the Sun and the Ibis seemed weird enough to warrant a visit to their temples, but time was against us and we set out for Assiut at dawn the following day.

Soon after leaving Minya two police cars joined us, one ahead and one astern; light-brown Muskovitch saloons. As on the previous day, scowling faces appeared at the rear window of the leading car; they must have suffered cricked necks, for at no period during that journey were we unobserved for even a moment. Many excellent photographs were missed since the risk involved by incurring the displeasure of the police at this stage of the journey was not worth taking. However the rear car was not able to see what was going on in the cab of our rear Land-Rover, so Anthony and Mike filmed whatever they felt to be of interest, including the road-blocks, bridge-guards, and groups of bedraggled local militia. Nick even took some excellent shots of an uncovered trainload of Russian tanks which passed on the rail beside us. Such shots were of little use to us, but the very presence of our limpet-like escort encouraged perversity.

The road to Luxor passes through Assiut, Sohag and Qena; all sizeable towns with crowded streets. As soon as the hovercraft were glimpsed, all other interests were forgotten and the masses closed in to touch and cry out in wonder at the strange machines. Without our escorts, I shudder to think how long the journey through Egypt would have taken, nor how long our patience and the vehicles' clutches would have lasted. The country between the towns lies lush and hazy on either side of the river, cotton and sugar cane, palms and water-wheels, merry lads paddling in the disease-ridden canals with their fine teeth flashing as they waved; some straining glazed young eyes to comprehend our weird burdens, for trachoma is no respecter of youth in these parts.

Between orange and citrus groves, muddled banks of pigeon-houses peeped above thorn hedges. A protracted argument with our day's dictator, à fat inspector named Farouk who never left his Muskovitch, eventually found him agreeing that the security of the U.A.R. would not be risked by his giving us permission to photograph these dovecots. Local village crops used to be thought to be aided in their growth and fertility by flocks of communally owned and housed pigeons kept in pagoda-like buildings made of clay. Hundreds of little doves live in these huts which resemble Gorgonzola cheeses. Clay pipes acting as entrance or exit holes protude from the domed roofs like so many porcupine quills. As we approached, clouds of birds fluttered upwards in alarm but many returned as we stopped to photograph them. Their droppings are thought to fertilise the local crops and even to affect the final size and quality of the fruits; they are also sold by the brace quite cheaply and are delicious with mealy corn and hot butter sauce. But the authorities are now discouraging their breeding since in fact they do more damage to crops than indirect good.

At the village of Samhud north of Qena we were flagged down by a khaki-clad policeman and our escort, having pulled in, waved us on airily. Surprised at this sudden and not entirely desired freedom, we carried on slowly and rather uncertainly,

Nick getting out our road maps for the first time since leaving Cairo. We came to a fork near Nag Hammadi and since it was not shown on our maps, tossed a piastre and went left. The graded murram surface soon degenerated into pot-holed muck, and sugar-cane closed in on either side. We met a farm cart pulled by mules whose ancient owner was as obstinate as they, and who made it plain to us that his mules were quite incapable of going into reverse even if he wanted them to. Peter suggested a couple of shots into the air with the automatic, but remembering that it was Nag Hammadi bridge, a few miles away, which had so recently been blown up by the Israeli commandos, I desisted and we began the painful business of reversing our entire convoy for at least half a mile down the windy pot-holed sugar-cane alleys till we at last came back to the fork. I swear the old mule man was happier than he had been for many a year and he waved a sugar-cane stalk deliriously as we departed to try our luck down the right hand fork.

It led to Qena through thick cane country where little railways wound between plantations and camels filled miniature rolling-stock with bundles of cane—their loads larger than themselves so that, as they moved, only their long ungainly legs were visible. Kene means 'the black country' for it was here that the sculptors of the Pharaohs mined the hard black stone found nowhere else in Egypt. Here, too, the Nile is only some sixty miles from the Red Sea and archaeologists say the river once flowed east to the sea through a narrow gorge which still exists. The clay of Qena is of superior quality and until recently all Egypt's water-wheel pots were fashioned here.

A long metal girder-bridge spans the Nile at Qena and is heavily guarded day and night by a series of sandbagged machine gun emplacements. A new escort awaited us by the barrier and greeted us quite pleasantly compared with his predecessor's opening grunts of acknowledgement. He had a tape-measure with which he measured the width of the larger trailer, and he clucked his tongue dubiously, shaking his head at us. Nick exclaimed that if we were transgressing Egypt's traffic laws regarding maximum widths allowed on the road, then it was a bit late in the day to do anything about it. But this wasn't the problem at all as the policeman explained. The bridge had been built mainly for the railway which ran across its left hand flank, and Egyptian lorries were all fairly narrow so the 'motor lane' of the bridge was not necessarily wide enough to take our trailers. This was very nearly a disaster, for although we found there was about half an inch to spare on either side of the trailer sideboards, the approach to the bridge was curved and equally narrow. Only by gargantuan efforts and the help of the bridge-guards with their slung automatics did we manage to manoeuvre the trailers onto the bridge itself; from then on it was only a matter of meticulous and painfully slow steering to keep vehicle and trailer dead centre on the loose wooden planks to avoid tearing the hovercraft on sharp metal girders from both sides. Sweating profusely and thanking the bridge-guards for their invaluable aid, we left hoping all Nile bridges were not to be like this one. We later rather wished they had been.

# CHAPTER 6

∾

## Rising Waters

There is a scruffy public lawn enclosed by low hedges outside the Luxor police-station which, if it were anywhere else, would be an ideal spot for murder, rape and theft. We bedded down on what appeared by the inadequate light of a street lamp to be the cleanest, least-spat-upon morsel of grass in this green. Charles, Nick and Peter then decided there was no need to suffer unduly in this nocturnal meeting-place of Luxor's entire mosquito population and so visited a dingy inn at the far side of the square which had been recommended by the escort who dropped us off after our journey from Qena. Whatever the police had found so attractive about the place must have been upstairs, for the dormitory-type quarters of the nether regions were dirty, smelled foul, and heaved with belching, snoring humanity who presumably harboured as many fleas as there were mosquitoes in our 'garden' camp. But the three of them managed to persuade the old proprietor to find three neighbouring beds with a window quite near.

Charles felt like some food and the two of us took a pony-cab to the more salubrious side of town noting as we passed, the illuminated pillars and low walls of the temple of Amon. We turned at random into the gay Saad Zaghoul street, where a small café—with a tantalising aroma of curry and oranges wafting from its open front—announced on a green placard 'Mensa Thebes Restaurant' and underneath, 'Friendly Advices for Students'. If its food was as full of imagination as its advertising, we thought the menu would prove entertaining. The young owner who spoke his own quaint brand of American, one Hussein Abdel-Radi, waited on some five tables, each seating four; anticipating every wish of his customers, he had a spontaneous line of amusing patter which included witty jabs at the establishment and the recent efforts of the war machine. The food was delicious and cheap.

After the meal we returned to the Nileside road which passes beneath the temple. From close by, the ruins look comparatively small and it is difficult to think of them as part of the greatest religious complex in the world. Only fifty-odd years ago the ruins lay hidden beneath a hill of dust and rubble, mud houses and even a small mosque; then a sewage drain was sunk from a hovel and struck what turned out to be the very top of one of the giant papyrus columns.

A bit further up the river bank is the imposing Winter Palace Hotel. Here we asked for Madame Youssaria, the local representative of the Ministry of Tourism, to whom we had an excellent introduction in the form of a bottle of pills from the Military Attaché in Cairo. He had told us she was extremely anxious to get these pills and indeed her ample face did light up when, after introducing ourselves, we produced the little bottle with the compliments of the sender. Unfortunately her joy was short-lived for the pills were apparently the wrong type. For half an hour we chatted her up, insisting that the tourist attraction value of having a hovercraft performing on the Nile in front of the temple of Luxor would be unprecedented—the old and the new meet in go-ahead Luxor; and think of the photographs her bureau could obtain with the magnificent background of the ruins for Egypt's first hovercraft performance.

Madame Youssaria was warming to the idea and even taking notes on our suggestions, when three short, fat men greeted her, ignoring us, and sat themselves down at our table. It is a fact that all regional security men in the U.A.R. appear to be short and fat, having hard little gimlet eyes and many large signet-rings which never remain still for a second. The overall effect is unpleasant, and although Madame Youssapof, as Charles insisted on calling her, plainly disliked these crude policemen, she agreed without query to all they were telling her and when they left, apologised to us for their manners and for the unfortunate fact that a demonstration of the hovercraft would not after all be possible for security reasons. The Egyptians are a charming people on the whole, but many of their officials seem to feel it their duty to be offensive.

On returning to the 'police lawn', I found Anthony and Mike sipping Horlicks beneath the street lamp. To check our lack of progress, we spread the large-scale map of the Nile out over the grass. Seen from source to estuary it was a daunting sight, especially since the map was at least eighteen feet long. We did not expect to leave Aswan until the 3rd March when the next steamer was due to depart, so owing to the Egyptians' 'no hovering' edicts, we would arrive on the Sudanese border at Wadi Halfa at least a week behind our schedule. This was not serious so long as the sandstorms, and later the rains, were not early.

As we squatted meditating over the out-size map, a police-officer in smart black uniform with Teutonic knee-length boots appeared with five khaki-clad underlings sporting automatic rifles. "You will go now to my room and take this chart with you. What do you do at this time of night in the darkness of these gardens that is so secret? You will explain your actions to my chief at once."

I think he really felt he'd made a major catch, as did the rifle-toting subordinates who bunched us and directed us to an office in the police building. Our maps were certainly not in microdot, our presence no well-kept secret, nor were the gardens in front of a police-station quite the best place to carry out espionage work. But the national undercurrent of suspicion was at work here in Luxor, where there was absolutely nothing to spy on or attack, as much as anywhere else, and even the 'chief' with whom we spent the next two hours needed a lot of persuasion before believing that we were engaged in a harmless journey up Father Nile. He told us that the hovercraft were a very good cover for our spying activities, that our radios were similar to those used by the Israelis, and that two of us were working for the imperialist forces still present in the Arab world and therefore obviously against the U.A.R. regime which leads the anti-royalists.

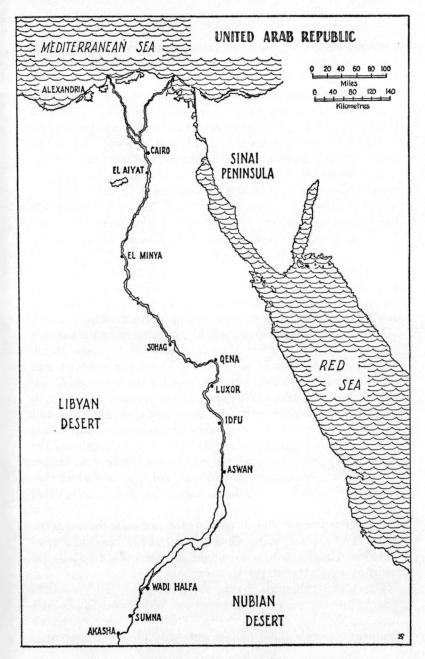

The United Arab Republic

I was not certain how he knew Peter and I worked in the Middle East, but assured him that our work had nothing to do with our political feelings.

The black-uniformed man drew our interrogator to one side with an air of menacing gravity and the latter asked us in harsh tones why our map—which was of all the Nile countries—only had grid co-ordinates for the U.A.R. and why so many pencil marks surrounded places like El Minya and Cairo with random figures scribbled in the margin. I explained as patiently as possible that the map-makers in Sudan and Uganda obviously hadn't got down to intimate survey-work before the British left those countries, whereas in Egypt mapping had been completed by the British Army whose maps were still used in the country. Also that the pencilled entries were records of our progress and so covered only the route we had already travelled. After much humming and Arab hawing we were permitted to leave without the map and warned that we were under close observation and any irregular behaviour would see us in severe trouble.

We left the office feeling much as I imagine most Russians do after a brush with their authorities; relieved to leave at all. Our imprisonment could be used as a handy blackmail lever in the event of the British Defence Ministry making sudden decisions over arms sales to the Israelis. An international incident always has small beginnings and often with as unwitting and unimportant participants as us. I remembered a minor 'war' which I had narrowly avoided sparking off between the Omanis and the People's Republic of Southern Yemen only a few months earlier.

My reconnaissance platoon had been assigned the task of capturing, preferably alive, bin Nuffl, the number two 'adoo' or rebel of the Dhofari guerillas, who had been reported living for a few days at the border village of Habarut between the Southern Yemen and Dhofar, and a close relation of the bin Nuffl, mentioned in chapter two, who sought aid from King Faizal and returned across the Empty Quarter by car.

The Mahri tribesmen live in the wild, dry country on both sides of the border, wandering between Yemen and Dhofar and ignoring the theoretical borderline. On the whole they favour Southern Yemen's claim to Habarut although the village oasis itself lies on the eastern side of the Wadi Habarut and so is in fact in Dhofar territory. The Sultan naturally considers it his village and garrisons a fort there with civilian askars, whilst eight hundred yards away on the west side of the same wadi, the Yemeni Army man another fort. It was not known which side of the frontier bin Nuffl was on, nor if he was for certain in the village of Habarut or perhaps being aided by the Yemenis in their fort. My commanding officer did not give me permission actually to cross the border, neither had he forbidden it, and who was to know why and how one Dhofari rebel should disappear of a dark night, when his normal movements were known to be highly erratic.

I was dropped with three men and machine-guns in a wadi several miles north of the village and the little Beaver plane returned twice more until there were some nine soldiers and a guide. We moved that night down to the village and the chief of the Sultan's askars met us as arranged by the well. He explained apologetically that his local spy had failed to tell him exactly where the rebel and his band were camping so he could not himself take us there. He suggested we wait until the next night, by when he would have the necessary information, but I told him this was impossible since bin Nuffl would soon learn of our presence from the wandering Mahri shepherds who could, and would, pick up our tracks the next morning when their flocks left the village. We would have to locate the informant and then go with him to bin Nuffl's hideout. The informant lived in the middle of the village and was the only Bait Kathiri there— the Bait Kathir being on unfriendly terms with the Mahri. The chief askar was not at all pleased with the idea of wandering through the village at night and possibly getting himself mixed up in a shooting match, so he assured me that his work lay within the walls of his fort and he had better return there forthwith. I in turn assured him that on the contrary his work was wherever the Sultan chose and as the Sultan's representative here he would be held responsible if bin Nuffl was not captured. Sullenly he led us through the sleeping village as silently as possible, for the sand was littered with dead palm branches from the trees above, and the place full of half-starving curs aching for something to snarl and bark at.

We stopped in a clearing with the stars glinting clear and large, the chief askar disappeared for some time and returned with a withered old leper whose features I could not make out in the dark. He spat continually as he whispered and since the sounds he made were comparable to those of an asthmatic pensioner from the Hebrides, I had to align my ear with his mouth in order to make head or tail of his conversation. My own guide was also Bait Kathir, so translated the gist of the old man's mutterings. His uncle had been killed five years back by bin Nuffl and he was an old man with no relatives to settle the blood score, so when he had heard his enemy was nearby he had at once told the askars in the hope that they would kill the hated bin Nuffl. Unfortunately bin Nuffl had only that afternoon left Habarut for an unknown destination together with his band of cut-throats. However he had also seen soldiers from the Yemeni fort, sometimes with an officer, visiting the village and talking to the villagers, exhorting them, he thought, to revolt. Indeed were we to wait overnight we would be almost certain to catch them in the act. I had heard similar tales from some of the askars on earlier routine visits to the fort, and so laid a careful ambush along the tracks leading to the village through the scrub on the other side of the wadi.

Some nagging thought prompted me to send a signal back to base to inform them of my altered intentions. The reply took some time to come, but it fortunately arrived before the Yemeni trespassers did. "The Sultan expressly forbids the seizure of personnel from P.R.S.Y. Return to base at once." So we left the village and I realised, ignorance being bliss, that to turn a blind eye on border incursions was preferable to risking a war. The incident made me painfully aware that unpleasant upheavals often have small beginnings. Ten years rotting in an Egyptian cell could so easily have resulted from our harmless map check in the Luxor public gardens.

We were to leave Luxor the next evening, so the police-officer informed us, and would be allowed to see the Valley of the Kings that day, but of course with a police escort tagging on too.

Whilst inspecting the mummy of Seti the First which had been dug up from its tomb and was lying forlorn and most unregally on a wooden board (with teeth and nails still partially visible), we met Alan and Jane, whom we had lifted from Alex to Cairo: they had reached Luxor by train and would be going on to Aswan by rail the next day. Poor old Alan looked on his last legs and the intense glaring heat didn't help. Our escort proved fairly knowledgeable on the tombs and their murals and, unlike the many other two-bit guides, whose only real expertise lay in the extraction of piastres from tourists, he was free; so we had quite a crowd of Russians following us and straining their thick necks to catch his quaint words of bastardised English.

After a confusing afternoon of Pharaohs, animal gods, mummies and tombs the most remarkable thing I noticed was the great similarity between the daily life of the Egyptian fellah of 4,000 years ago, when Thebes, Karnak and Luxor were at the zenith of their power, and his counterpart of today. The same dress, food, and customs, the same water-wheels and the same poverty-inspired toil, day in day out without respite. Only in their religious and social standing are things much changed; now they can identify themselves with their God and their rulers. The ancient Pharaohs called them the sechetti, then they became known as fellahin, 'those who work on the land'. They still work on the land, but now their taxes are bearable and the rewards of labour tangible.

We left golden Luxor before sunset and had soon passed Silsileh where the Nile is at its narrowest, being only some eighty-five yards across at low flood. It was thought by the early Pharaohs to be far the best place for communing with the spirits or gods of the Nile, for after all there was nowhere else you could at one time be so near both banks. In times of drought and famine, the Pharaohs would drive here in splendour from nearby Luxor and, throwing scrolls with written petitions or sacrificial white oxen into the waters, they would beg for a high flood season to come; one likes to think at this stage of thunder-clouds bursting spumes of dark deluge over the towering crags of distant Abyssinia's Highlands, to thunder down the country's mysterious river gorges, running on through the swamps to

Khartoum, through the deserts to Silsileh and the parched fields of Egypt—so that all might praise and wonder at the might of the Pharaoh whom even the Nile obeyed.

From Silsileh by night to Kom Ombo, where the streets seethed with Egypt's troops, whether reserves, recruits or men on leave from the Suez front, we could not tell, for the escort took pains to speed our passage through the town and its vicinity. A friendly policeman in Aswan a couple of days later told us in a confiding fashion that Kom Ombo was a base of great importance and that "the Israeli soldiers would desert in thousands were they to know the strength of Egypt's reserves in the Republic's stronghold."

Kom Ombo is also the site of an ambitious resettlement scheme for some seventy thousand homeless Nubians whose villages have been inundated by the rising waters of Lake Nasser. What we saw of the lines of low unimaginative block-houses which form the basis of the scheme led us to feel sceptical over the Nubians' reported reaction to their move. After centuries of life by the Nile, eking an existence from fish and a few crops by the water's edge, they were to be turned overnight into farm-workers and cotton-pickers. Their old dried mud houses had a style of their own which was pleasing to the eye and no two houses ever looked similar though they blended easily with the rugged background of sand and water. Now they were to settle in rows of uniformly constructed brick huts with a new set of rules on how to live, when and where to wash and ablute, and even to suffer periodic inspections of their homes by health officers. Freud would doubtless have quite a bit to say on the probable effects of such a metamorphosis on the poor Nubians.

But it's all in the cause of progress and the Aswan Dam, which is causing all the heartbreak, is also scheduled to produce an extra million acres of arable land in Egypt on its completion. Unfortunately it looks as though the fellahin are second to none at propagating their species and the country's population will need more than an added million acres to contain it after a couple of years at the present rate of growth.

Not far from Kom Ombo we came to a road-block of unprecedented size and thoroughness. Even our escort cars were looked at carefully, our mentors having to produce their identity cards,

though they were obviously well-known to the officials there. For
the first time since leaving Britain the radios, arms, spare engines,
and cameras were all inspected individually and the serial
numbers recorded. We awaited the verdict of the discussions
which then took place for over an hour, with numerous telephone
calls, in the officials' booth, and gloomily agreed between ourselves that this must be the road-block where all Europeans
were stopped and turned back about which we had been told
by various disappointed tourists on our way down. But no, once
again our unknown sponsors in the Ministry of Tourism smoothed
our path and we cruised triumphantly through the barriers soon
after midnight.

A hub cap popped off a trailer wheel, spewing steaming grease
onto the road; the brake system had become jammed and we had
been driving, probably since Luxor, with the brake drums bind-
ing; both wheel hubs were extremely hot and one of the shoes
cracked and jammed within its housing. We stripped off the
entire brake system and hoped that no steep hills would come our
way. With regreased hubs, and ignoring the protesting squeak
which set in as soon as we moved off, we carried on wearily to
Aswan over fifty miles of appalling roads with pot-holes like
Biggin Hill bomb craters.

Some time before dawn we arrived at the Aswan Police Headquarters, a grim grey building with a big courtyard in its centre.
The entrance, through a stone passageway, was narrow, but we
pushed the trailers through separately and set up camp in the
dirty yard. All around were barred doors of cells with curious
prisoners scrutinising us. There was the normal assortment of
petty thieves and drunks, and some smartly suited executive
types as well. From somewhere inside the building hysterical
screams echoed from time to time and Nick commented
cryptically on the Spanish Inquisition, suggesting that torture
always comes hand in hand with dictatorships and republics.
I felt it more likely that some poor soul was mourning the loss
of a relative in a recent traffic accident. The screams continued
during the night. Forty or fifty bedraggled citizens, some in
khaki shirts but most in flowing white djellabias, arrived in dribs
and drabs at eight in the morning and, when their names were

97

shouted out from a cell converted into an arms store, they each drew an old rifle, a handful of rounds, and an empty ammunition belt. Their shouts and coughs made sleep impossible, particularly as each and every one came round our mosquito nets with loud comments of speculation over Baker and Burton, so we watched as they performed some rudimentary rifle drills in a perfunctory and entirely unco-ordinated fashion, then lined up in column and marched off with arms swinging lustily and quite out of step. We watched in silence from under our nets; if these were Egypt's reserves, God help them if they ever met up with the Israeli forces.

There isn't much to see in Aswan other than the amusing sight of Russian wives trying to buy groceries for their engineer husbands. None of them seemed to speak a word of Arabic but all had obviously been briefed on the swindling prowess of Egyptian shopkeepers. Juxtaposition resulted, both parties determined to get the best of even the smallest deal. Assuan means market in Arabic, and the inhabitants have a very fine marketing sense.

Peter, Charles and Nick decided that a second night listening to the screams and thumpings of the territorial units at the police compound was a bad idea and found accommodation on board a floating hotel-boat with minute but clean bunks and mosquito-free cabins. Even though our vehicles were with the police, I still didn't feel the kit was completely safe, and the photographers felt the same about their equipment, so I issued cotton-wool from the first aid box, and we settled down to a deep sleep ignoring the miscellaneous disturbances till dawn, when the first of the civvy soldiers arrived back. They must have been on a fairly long march for they were still arriving in twos and threes at midday, looking quite incapable of lifting rifles to shoulders, let alone firing straight. We washed and breakfasted on the boat, rather wishing we too had spent the night there as mosquito bites itched maddeningly.

There is a drive of some twelve miles from the town of Aswan to Shellal where a crude and very temporary landing stage serves to let passengers on and off the tramp steamers which go to Wadi Halfa. But neither the landing platform nor the barges towed by the steamer are built to take cars, even small cars. As usual tickets and reservations were never acknowledged till the last moment, when everything was done in a rush. Till then no-one would help find a cabin nor even confirm that there was one available. But we could ill-afford to wait till the last minute, for it was going to require serious thought and probably even alterations to the deck structure of the passenger barge if our machines were to fit on board at all.

With the unco-ordinated aid of an amorphous gaggle of Arabs, five Germans and two hippy Americans—who thought the hover-craft were 'dead cool'—we managed to drive the Land-Rovers up two wooden planks onto the deck and, scraping their canopies on the metal struts of the upper decking, to manhandle them around steel bollards and wire hawsers. Both hovercraft followed and there was a moment of great anguish when part of the wooden gangway ramps cracked and split under a trailer wheel. Only the phenomenal strength of the Arab crewmen lifting both hovercraft and trailer on the side where the wheel was suspended over the dirty water of Lake Nasser, saved Burton from an untimely launching and its trailer from probable loss.

Baker was the last on and never quite made it; there just wasn't room—even after we had removed several metal spars which supported the upper deck—so one trailer wheel and part of the hovercraft protruded well over the side of the barge for the rest of the journey. Any passenger wishing to cross from one barge to the other had to climb over the bonnet of a Land-Rover and crawl beneath the tow-hook of a trailer. Since the floor was coated in sheep dung, oil, and orange-skins, most of the passengers had no desire to make the trip, so we left our kit in the vehicles quite safely for once.

The water used for cooking, washing and drinking on board was all scooped up in buckets tied to ropes, and was, even in mid-lake, spiced with green and brown algae which lent a sewage-like quality to its texture, and on reflection, generations of steamers with no inbuilt latrines had indeed been plying these waters. Our water sterilisers came into their own and the Nubian deck hands got a kick out of pumping them as vigorously as possible, so that pots of sterilised tea were soon being bought by

99

all and sundry. Even the hippies came down from the top deck of the cattle barge, where they had taken over a shady nook beneath a hatch and where they smoked odd-smelling black stuff and stroked one another. We sterilised some tea for them which they seemed to appreciate. They enquired what we were up to and when Peter told them, one of their number—an American girl with long dark hair and moccasins—said wonderingly, "They're doing their own thing all right, but it sure takes all types to make a world." I felt like putting her right—we were the squares; her lot the drop-outs, but then it's really all a matter of which way you look at it so I kept quiet.

Bullfrogs and the usual Arab chanting vied with the leaden heat to keep us from sleeping that night. Sunset had been rich in subtle patterns and soft colours of every hue, the view ethereal and calming. Empty plains with gaunt, black rock-formations stretch away from the lake on both sides to form the deserts of Libya and Arabia. The boat stopped soon after dusk, though there was no good reason for doing so, and anchored in a rocky inlet. Here wolves and hyena howled wildly and a sliver of pearl-white moon chased the brilliant stars in a sky of midnight blue. Moon shadows danced crazily and promised mystery amongst the jagged rocks where once the men of Kush held strange ceremonies. We joined the hippies on their roof and lay back to think the longing thoughts which come in such places. The Arabs too fell silent and the barges squeaked only slightly where the hemp lashed them together.

Charles had discovered one of our whisky bottles to be accessible amongst the miscellaneous gear in one of the Land-Rovers, so we drank and sang Scottish ballads on the roof to the tune of the hippy's guitar. Beneath us, in the silent dancing waters, lurked the microscopic deathbug bilharzia. Bilharziasis is a highly unpleasant, and in its later stages, agonising sickness to contract. There is now a cure, which is a course of painful deep stomach injections, but as yet no form of prevention other than keeping even the smallest drop of water from the skin. Before the vast irrigation schemes of Egypt in the Delta and of Sudan in the Gezira, bilharzia was little known. As soon as the perennial irrigation systems were introduced, and canals, which carried drinking-water, were no longer allowed to drain off, bilharzia and various other parasites increased alarmingly. By 1932, some sixty per cent of the populace had hook-worm. In the centre of the river, where there is a fairly strong current, the parasites cannot survive; they are found where the water is more or less stagnant, as in all the canals, and where water reeds clog the river. Even spray from a paddle can contain the parasites and as soon as the little worms feel the spray evaporating, they will dig into the skin to escape the heat of the sun, burrowing through unbroken skin with ease. They then make their way to the liver where they feed and breed a new cycle of worms leaving the body in the exreta. Once back in the water, the worms use water snails as their host bodies, and are at this stage most open to destruction by spray deterrents.

We had been warned in London of the deadly little water-borne parasites, but seeing the inviting depths of moon-silvered waters and feeling unduly merry, we dived off the deck rails and floated in the cool lake. The skipper and his crew came running from their cabins when they heard the splashes and lined the boat railings in their white pyjamas (worn by day as well as night). Two of them removed a life belt from its rusty housing, but discovered its rope had at some stage been removed, probably for tying to the water bucket. When they realised it was only the English hover people gone for a swim, they shrugged and returned to their berths. Although there was no reason why crocodiles should keep away from Lake Nasser, we felt they would be asleep and aground at that time of night, and so swam a mile or so towards the other bank, coming of a sudden on a small fishing-boat rocking gently in the slight desert breeze. A dark shape sprang from the floor of the boat brandishing a weapon of some sort and challenging us. The spirits of the lake are much feared by sinners and judging by the palpitations of the boatman, he didn't consider himself an angel. We hastened to assure him that we were no apparitions, but declined his invitation to come aboard; maybe he now thought we were Israeli frogmen on our way to the Dam.

Nick developed bilharzia on returning to Britain a month later and rather wished he had resisted the temptations to swim;

but in the Sudan there were occasions when there was no choice but contact with the water, and indeed, for four weeks we drank nothing but unfiltered Nile. We passed the El Sibu and Amada temples on their recently-raised bases and on the second night saw the distant lights of the workers at the new Abu Simbel site. Otherwise no sign of life save the occasional deserted village half-submerged, where only a few mangy cats survive.

An old man, whose son said he was of the Ingassana tribe, from the south of Khartoum, approached us the morning we reached Wadi Halfa and asked us in classical Arabic if we could supply him with a hypodermic and clean needle. Ours was down beneath God knows how much kit in one of the vehicles, so Nick suggested the hippies would be bound to have one in frequent use. But when the old man whimpered that it was a matter of life and death, we found our first aid box and also a retired doctor. The latter spoke English, and after injecting the leathery hip of the man, explained that there are literally thousands of such bilharzia patients who are meant to inject themselves weekly or have their family do it for them. There are vast areas in the Sudan without hospitals and there is not all that room in the existing ones, not that this reflects badly on the government, for the Sudan is an enormous country, with only four million scattered inhabitants, and communications are always difficult and, during the rains, impossible.

We came to Wadi Halfa early on the 5th March. It looks isolated when first seen on the map, since deserts surround it for hundreds of miles on every side, and as no really motorable road leads to it, it depends on the Nile for its very existence. The people here are the happiest people in the world, though they have every reason to be the saddest, and we, too, felt a weight off our minds as we left Egypt and its troubles behind us, and entered Africa's largest and most mysterious land.

# CHAPTER 7

∞

## *Fire and Water*

The grey-blue waters of Lake Nasser lie over an Atlantis of the Nubian Desert. Wadi Halfa—Arabic for grassy valley—was only recently a favourite tourist haunt of Europeans and Americans who flocked to see the unique life and customs of the oasis dwellers, living as they did in the midst of a sweltering desert, nursing a few acres of fertility, clinging to the Nile, and encompassed by vast areas of black and ochre nothingness where camel bones gleam on long forgotten tracks. Here luxury steamers used to moor by stone quays beneath lofty palm and neem trees. Flocks of desert snipe and wood pigeon would wheel and flutter over gardens where fruit and flowers of every kind grew in bewildering profusion. Now all lies buried by Lake Nasser, all but the solitary spire of a minaret, and even this will have disappeared in a year as the Aswan Dam fills up.

The Egyptians are the beneficiaries of the offending dam that caused all this, not the Sudanese, and certainly not the Wadi Halfans. True, the Egyptian High Dam Authorities gave the Sudanese some fifteen million pounds compensation for their land loss, but little of this came the way of the Wadi Halfans, the people who lost their homes. They were sent to Khashm al Girba in far-away Kassala Province, to work on a great new government agricultural project. This was originally intended to be worked by some Kassala nomads who were to be settled and trained as farmers. But the nomads have proved difficult to settle, let alone turn into farmers, so the government had decided to kill two birds with one stone and send the dispossessed but hard-

working Wadi Halfans to Khashm al Girba to start off the
farming scheme. The Kassala nomads would, they hoped, be
attracted soon enough once they saw productivity bring material
wealth to the ex-Wadi Halfans.

The whole eviction and resettlement project had been con-
ceived and carried through with complete lack of regard to
the feelings and hopes of the Wadi Halfans themselves, and the
Military Government of 1958, already unpopular, dug its own
grave when it sent soldiers to Wadi Halfa to evict and entrain
the protesting townsfolk.

The friendly Chief Customs Officer, Mr. Moyadeen, had spent
his youth in the old town and remembered the troubled
times of the eviction. He explained why there was still any
habitation at all in the Wadi Halfa area. When the soldiers had
forced the last dwellers from the doomed town, a few of the
more die-hard families—all Nubians—had refused to join the
resettlement convoys. Even though their township was lost to
them they would not leave their beloved desert by the side of
the river they knew so well. They were sure that life would not
be worth living on the distant plains of Kassala and would prefer,
if necessary, to die of starvation, so long as they could stay in
their homeland. So they built temporary dwellings some eight
miles upstream—near the river so that they could drink, fish,
and wash. Their little shanty town was also close to the desert
terminal of Kitchener's old rail to Khartoum, so a few travellers
still called with whom some trade could be conducted. Each
year at the flood season the water has risen and been held at
its new level by the distant barrier at Aswan. Before the floods
come each time, the shanty-dwellers—from the headman to the
humblest fisherman—have had to move their homes and belongings back to higher ground before the relentless waters. Virtually
nothing will grow in the soft sand so they subsist on a basic
diet of fish. Remembering Sir Winston Churchill's wartime words
'Bricks and mortar do not make a city but the people that live
in it', the Nubians have tenaciously held on through the difficult
years when the government failed to recognise the presence of
any habitation at Wadi Halfa, let alone support it. But the
military government did not last long and with a change of

national administration and policy, aid came in and the little shanty town began to thrive in its own small way, waiting only for the day when the waters cease to rise and the townsfolk can once again live in their own static homes on the banks of the Nile.

The men who have stayed behind in the shanty town have every reason to be hurt and embittered by their treatment, yet they are not. They are proud men, these frontier Nubians, and describe themselves as the Guardians of the Border; for they still mistrust the land-hungry Egyptians and I feel that the natural and ethnic frontier of the Sudan should be at Aswan as it once used to be. If they were to leave Wadi Halfa, they point out, what would there be to stop the Egyptians encroaching to the south?

The total rise in the water level has so far been 158 metres, and this July the final proposed level, increasing the depth by a further twenty-six metres, will be achieved. The site for a permanent new Wadi Halfa has already been plotted and new industries planned, based on the terminal station of the railway from Khartoum, with a shipping canal now being dug to connect the fully risen lake to the railway station.

Until this canal is finally completed and the waters cease to rise, the steamers coming from Aswan will still have to beach in the shallows at the edge of the lake as they do now, disgorging their various goods and passengers into rowing boats for the last short passage to the shore.

No-one had warned us of this novel method of disembarking, and the Nubian crew observed our expressions of growing perplexity and dismay with delight; they knew what was coming— that without their well-tipped aid, our vehicles and therefore ourselves would remain marooned on board. There was a drop from deck to water of several feet, and the water's depth was a further four feet where the boat had beached. I left the solution of this problem to the ever-practical Peter and hastened to clear our papers and goods with the customs officer, a man who would have been the height of official elegance were it not for the layers of fine white dust on his pressed khaki suit, as on everything else in Wadi Halfa. He drove me over some two miles of bumpy desert in an ancient Dodge to the present site of the shanty town. We met the commissioner, Sayyid Ibrahim, who resembled the Sanders of the River I remembered from school-days, complete with ebony cane and light-brown sun helmet. His greeting was effuse; he had been awaiting us for the last two weeks, he said, and had even met two of the steamers with a civic reception party to welcome us. He showed me a copy of the *Daily Telegraph* headed 'Concern for Nile Expedition'. Nothing had been heard of our whereabouts for two weeks and the authorities had become alarmed. We sent off telegrams to assure the Foreign Office and our families of our continued existence.

The commissioner had also heard that the President and entire Supreme Court of the Sudan were to attend our proposed hover-ing demonstration in Khartoum, which had been fixed in our absence for the 14th March. This gave us just a week to hover some thousand miles of Nile including three of the river's notorious cataracts. This was hardly long enough even without time allowed for mishaps, but there would be no harm in having a go, so I told the commissioner we would leave as soon as the craft were ready.

His house, though temporary had simple character. The wooden front-door, like that of most Wadi Halfan homes, was moved with the furniture though the rest of the house was left at each successive move of the hungry waters – there being no wood to be had for hundreds of miles.

Colourful hardboard murals depicting Wadi Halfa as it was before the waters rose decorated the walls of the sitting-room; they had been painted by a local artist shortly before the Wadi Halfans were evicted from their old town. The murals helped us to conceive the medley of greens of the orchards and the merry bustle of the towns-folk, so difficult to visualise now that all was submerged. The room was well supplied with chairs, for unlike the homes of the other Arab desert dwellers I have visited, the Nubians treat chairs as necessities rather than luxuries.

After delicious Nubian coffee and the local brand of sherbert served by the pretty, and unusually emancipated, wife of the commissioner, I returned to the lakeside to find the expedition on terra firma and Charles hard at work fitting propellers and wind-ducts to the drive engines. To get everything off the barge without damaging anything had been a major feat involving partial dismantling of the barge's side rails, heavy tips paid to a number of rotund but muscular Nubians, and an ingenious system of pulleys devised by Peter. Added to these was a large amount of luck, for the pulleys snapped at the crucial moment and a trailer complete with hovercraft, had gone thundering down the two metal ramps, and into the lake with a cloud of spray. As the wheels had kept in the runnels of the ramps, and the bed of the lake was fairly firm, no damage was done, except to Peter's pride. He recovered his engineering reputation by lowering the second craft smoothly by a veritable spider's web of ropes and counter-pulleys.

During our stay at Wadi Halfa we were never short of volunteer helpers aching to lend a hand, and since the Land-Rovers spent much of the time deeply bogged in the treacherous sand by the lakeside, these eternally grinning giants with their rhythmic chanting came in very handy.

Once propeller units were fixed, the five-gallon fuel tanks were filled with haphazardly prepared two-stroke mixture, and the six engines started up with remarkable little fuss considering the snow, salty water, and fine dust that they had been bared to over the last two weeks.

The leading edges of the propellers were strengthened by metal strips, but the dust might well chew these up and our supply of spare props was of necessity limited. The Neoprene skirts were of a newer and stronger type than those of the standard Hawk, but had only been tested on the smooth surface of Hoverair's little quarry pool.

Britain is holding its own in the field of large passenger-carrying hovercraft, and leads the world in the research and variety of its small crop-spraying and pleasure craft, but methods of strengthening and repairing the skirts of small craft vary as much as the skirt designs themselves and are usually based on water-resistant adhesives considerably stronger than the material being mended. Hoverair had been experimenting with the liberal use of pop rivets for repairing the seams, and strengthening the material where it was most liable to stress as on the sides of the leading edge of the skirt.

The smaller the craft, the more delicate the question of load dispersal. With only one 250 c.c. motor-cycle engine providing the total lifting power of each Hoverhawk, it was essential that a more or less perfect air-cushion be formed beneath the craft to give maximum lift without the engine requiring full thrust. This meant careful stowage of the bulky photographic equipment, radios, and of course the three four-gallon cans of fuel which travelled on the passenger's seat in Baker and gave the hover 'convoy' an extra 105 miles range without being refuelled from the Land-Rovers. We intended to average some twenty-five miles an hour using two and a half gallons an hour.

With much revving of engines and showers of fine sand from beneath the inflated skirts, Baker and Burton slid down the beach and away over the dawn-chilled waters of the lake with hardly a ripple to mark their passage. I drove Baker, Charles the newer, but somewhat slower, Burton, with Anthony's head poking out of the cockpit as he recorded the scene in Eastman-colour.

The lake was so wide, and the enclosing granite hills so uniform, that I could see no break in the horizon to head for. Burton soon dwindled behind into a fast diminishing speck only visible when the rays of the morning sun sparkled from its fibreglass hull, and rather than lose Charles for the rest of the day, I circled slowly to the east and north until heading back towards him. Now the gap between us closed with surprising speed for there was no sound and no sensation of movement, just the faint pull on the steering wheel as a breeze caught the fins. It was a novel feeling, quite unlike any other dimension of propulsion, and exaggerated by the vast and lonely lake. Charles flashed by at alarming speed, Anthony using up hundreds of feet of celluloid. He had always been cynical about the capabilities of the craft and was now making hay while the sun shone, and the hovercraft hovered.

There was a single rev counter on the control panel and close by it a lever with three positions, left or right to give the revolutions of the drive engines, centre to indicate the lift engine. Any attempt at lowering the revs of the latter had to be countered by more thrust on the drive units, but the converse was also true to a lesser extent, and so by careful manipulation of the throttle controls during a long journey, undue strain on all power units could be avoided.

Gaunt black rocks moved past the cockpit windows, weirdly fragmented and in violent contrast to the yellow beaches which connected them with the water. No shadows anywhere after nine in the morning, and the sun unquestionable master over everything that moved in this uncompromising land through which we coasted with wonder and the unspoken fear that a breakdown of any kind could well prove fatal so far from help.

A Hoverhawk must land; it cannot stop in midstream, lower itself into the water, and hope to start off again, for once the skirt is filled with water the lift engine will no longer suffice to clear it. A 'purge' or pump is needed, and this has only recently been fitted to the latest designs of Hawk. Stopping for any reason calls for a slightly sloped bank or, better still, a beach on which to land. A fact which had us eyeing the banks almost subconsciously for good potential landing-sites during the ensuing weeks.

In a landscape devoid of greens the palms of Sumna startled us, their fruitful crowns still visible above the water and accompanied more often than not by the tapering spires of once-proud mosques and little towers, from where the village faithful, and faithless, were once, not so long ago, called to prayer. Soon they will be completely covered and their mudbrick structure will crumble in a short passage of time. They were formed from Nile mud and so return to their former shapeless existence after briefly helping man to express himself to his Maker, for reasons of gratitude and pride, loneliness and fear.

Sumna was one such relic of Nubian oasis life, with the interesting difference that some forty villagers still lived there, and cheered, waving wildly and running along their little beach, as we passed. They must have thought we were motor-boats and neighbouring Wadi Halfa had once sported several of these so we caused no wonder, though had we drifted ghost-wise onto their beach and settled softly in the sand, big white eyeballs would no doubt have rolled in the delightful curiosity these Nubians have for all that's new.

Charles was keeping close records of fuel consumption and, with the aid of a pocket anemometer, the ever-changing wind speeds. The reactions of the engines to the strain of carrying maximum weight capacity in such high temperatures were also of importance, and were noted for the Ministry of Technology's eventual evaluation. The actual positioning of the reserve tanks affected the steering considerably and initially caused consternation, when in midstream the hovercraft would tend to waltz. Once this had been corrected by trimming out the two craft, Charles could maintain an easy twenty-five m.p.h. in Burton, carrying Anthony and all his photographic paraphernalia, whilst I took the fuel in Baker, strapped to the passenger seat, with a feed-pipe coming through from the engine compartment. As the fuel load lessened through the day, so I edged over in my seat towards the centre of the craft, for it soon became easy to feel when the trim was upset.

Our intention had been to reach Akasha, a fairly substantial riverside village sufficiently elevated to be unaffected by the rise of Lake Nasser, and to camp the night there awaiting the arrival on the 8th of the Land-Rovers and fuel.

Akasha was 150 miles from Wadi Halfa along the now submerged track which used to run beside the river. By river, the distance differs little from that of the old track, and fuel calculations were not difficult, but overland no-one had known where the 'new' road ran, that is, no-one at the Sudanese representative institutes in England, and several Sudanese I had asked, including the Ambassador had doubted that there was a road at all.

When one of Baker's drive engines gave up the ghost at about midday, and the repairs looked like taking some time, we were not unduly worried since it was very doubtful that the Land-Rovers would be able to keep to their side of the schedule and were more likely to reach Akasha sometime on the 9th, which would give us ample time to fix the engine and hover the remaining hundred miles the next day.

I fixed the position of our night camp as somewhere fairly close to the site of the Second Cataract, roughly where the Temple of Bohain is marked on local maps. It was an eerie spot and though the mighty falls no longer roared in perpetual but ever-changing notes of violence, the day's stiff breeze rose during the night and moaned fitfully through the crouching valleys of lurking shapes, rising to a high whine of impending menace. The air was full of stinging sand and our hair with a fine grit. Two of our cooking-pots and an assortment of bits and pieces left the area of the camp fire during the night and must have travelled far over the next two days of sandstorm. Only in the cockpits of the craft could one rest one's eyes from the blinding dust. The wind cracked our lips and made eyelids sore, retinas were bloodshot from tiny wounds inflicted by the flying grit.

There were still the ruins of an old building or two further down-stream from our camp; relics of Bohain from whence the Kings of Nubia once ruled an empire which included Egypt and parts of Libya, and stretched far south of Khartoum's present site. Tirhaka and his son Pianki, the only Nubians to truly turn the tables on the Pharoahs, were masters of Egypt in about 750 B.C., forming the twenty-fifth Dynasty of Egypt, their vassals travelling to the Bohain Temple to pay homage. But the Egyptians soon reconquered the Nubians and ruled the deserts here until the Christians came. We saw no traces of past glory, for the sands conceal all in time; traces of the Stone Age lay just beneath our feet as did remnants of Kitchener's campaigns. When Aswan grew in size and importance Bohain, no longer the vital linking-point between Egypt and Sudan, faded into insignificance, though it was long to remain the jumping-off point for military campaigns in both directions. The Pharoahs used it during the Middle and New Kingdoms, the Turks, and the British in their days of omnipotence, and the slave and ivory traders for as long as they had their being. Nineteenth-century Anglo-Egyptian rule and the railhead to Khartoum on the east bank shifted the last vestiges of influence from Bohain, and then Wadi Halfa had its brief period of glory, being, with Port Sudan, the greatest trading port of the Sudan.

The great temple of Bohain can still be seen in some of its

former splendour resurrected in the 'Wadi Halfa' Museum in Khartoum, together with two temples from the Sumna area, and one from Kasha, twenty-five miles north of the old Wadi Halfa. The saving of these buildings and other important relics from the Wadi Halfa area, was mainly due to the dedicated archaeologist Sayyid Naj Madun who still lives in Wadi Halfa and whom we interviewed during our stay there. He founded the Sudan Antiquity Service and generally sounded the warning bells about the effects of the High Dam flooding as early as 1956. He obtained financial support through U.N.E.S.C.O. and, by 1960, as many as sixteen archaeological teams from all over the world were at work on the removal and restoration of Wadi Halfa relics. Four teams are still working, but the Nubian Campaign completed its aims by November 1968, having saved over ninety per cent of all the buildings and relics of archaeological value in the area.

The winds blew without respite and the blue skies to which we had become accustomed deserted us; the world was grey, and at times dirty brown, as if some gigantic spiralling sand-devil had enveloped the region. The lake itself resembled a sea, the more so since the far bank was no longer visible, and white seahorses flecked the restless grey expanse. Waves of some two feet high were breaking on the rockier shores, no smaller than those off Brighton's beaches on a gusty day. Charles tuned the radio to the pre-set channel at eight o'clock, after a dismal breakfast of Horlicks iron rations and filtered Nile water, and almost at once heard Peter's distorted tones, "Hallo Nile, this is Rover, Radio Check, Over." Charles fiddled minutely with the clarifier knob and soon had Peter's voice coming clear and identifiable, despite the disturbed atmospherics, from some distant spot on the far and now invisible bank.

Peter sounded tired and annoyed. He told us in succinct and bitter tones just what the Nubians could do with their bloody sands and their even bloodier guides, and went on to describe the road party's progress to date—a chapter of disasters.

Having watched Burton and Baker roar off at speed till they faded into the distant orange waters, the two vehicles set off to Wadi Halfa to collect a guide promised us by the Shell represen-

Burton speeds upstream near Malakal through the floating islands of
water hyacinth.

The townsfolk at Malakal watch the arrival of the strange
'white aeroplane'.

A village on the Duk.

Ebony walking-stick makers of Bor. Still using Stone Age methods of drilling, they fashion the handles from hippo teeth.

tative the day before, the empty hovercraft trailers jolting behind
on the rough unsurfaced tracks. The guide turned out to be a
pitch-black Halfan named Ali bin Something-or-Other whose
English was quite reasonable but confined to all the wrong
things since, though he knew such terms as 'a very fine landscape', he was not capable of exclaiming 'left', 'right', 'in so many
miles', or even giving vague time estimates. Since he was expecting four Sudanese guineas for his aid as far as Akasha, Peter
was disgusted at his performance and soon gave up even bother-
ing to consult him.

Within two or three miles of Wadi Halfa, the sandy track
petered out and gave way to a series of partially distinguishable
tyremarks, half-buried by sand drifts through which the Rovers
roared and slithered their way in four-wheel drive and second
gear. The trailers with their little wheels did nothing to help,
but the oft recurring temptation to discard them had to be denied
as there was no telling when they would become indispensable.
By midday the heat had become hardly bearable and halts were
made whenever a hard gravel seam made it practical to stop.
Stopping anywhere else meant considerable strain on the clutch
whilst trying to get going again. The diesel machine was overheating with alarming frequency, and they soon decided that
rather than risk permanent damage to the engine they would
halt until dusk when it should become cooler.

Charles told Peter that excessive heat was something the
hovercraft party had not been suffering from, and the latter
replied that by his reckoning the vehicles were a good thirty
miles or more east of the river well into the bowl of the desert
and so not only caught the full reflected heat of the barren
land mass, but had no cooling river breeze to alleviate things.

The first vehicles to have travelled south from Wadi Halfa
after the riverside track had been submerged must have tried to
keep as close to the river as possible, but found, as did our Land-
Rovers, that a range of broken black hills stretches east from the
very edge of the risen waters for as far as forty miles in places,
with very few motorable routes running through them. We had
been told that a good guide could drive to Akasha, winding his
way through a series of interconnecting valleys, and never go

more than four or five miles east of the river, driving by night when the sands are cooler and harder and using stars or moon as his guide. The tracks of these local experts could be followed only at considerable risk, since in a couple of days they became invisible under the windblown sand in many places, and in the midst of those inhospitable winding valleys it was too easy to get permanently lost or bogged.

During the night the Land-Rovers struggled further south, with frequent forced diversions to the east as shadowy hills blocked the way. The channels of deep sand running between the rock formations were the only route and fortunately gravel seams crossed these channels at intervals. If sufficient speed was obtained on these hard stretches to carry vehicles and trailers through the next sand sea, all was well. However, gravity was not always on their side, for rolling dunes had to be climbed or traversed and in such places they toiled for many hours with shovels and tow ropes. They had completed seventy miles by midnight though only half of that could be counted as progress to the south, owing to their detours to the east, and the rising wind was whipping up the dust to make visibility difficult for the vehicle lights became ineffective in the swirling murk. The new Land-Rover was used with increasing frequency to drag the other from drifts and some hours before dawn, its clutch packed up completely, having been slipping and smelling for some time.

Dawn broke on the 8th to find them a sorry sight; huddled in the vehicle cabins in sleeping bags, sand everywhere, in eyes, hair, engines and food.

So Peter's tones of resignation over the wireless were understandable. He could have no real idea how far it was to Akasha, nor whether the track would improve or worsen. There was, therefore, no guarantee that they would ever make Akasha whether the winds dropped or not. For the hovercraft to cruise south with no assurance that fuel would arrive at their destination would be foolish, so we decided to cut our losses and for both parties to make their way back to Wadi Halfa. There was always the rail or road to Khartoum so we could still make the all-important demonstration on the 14th, and start our journey up the White Nile on schedule.

Charles discovered that Baker's right drive engine had a blown piston head which would need a particular type of spanner to fix, one which for all his supply of tools and spares, he didn't have. We decided to return in Burton, fetch the tools in question from the Shell representative in Wadi Halfa, a man of limitless resources, and leave Anthony with the lame Baker in our absence. I felt the end had come during the hair-raising journey back to Wadi Halfa, for the waves seemed to tower over the little cockpit and the slow windscreen wipers took their time to clear each successive deluge so that Charles was driving partially blind for much of the time. His confidence in his mini-craft was total. He chuckled delightedly as a series of three-foot waves took the Hawk sideways and rocked it violently. Incredibly the lift engine purred on smoothly and the craft maintained its 'hump' — the term used to describe the point at which friction between skirt and water is minimal and so drag does not interfere with forward propulsion.

With compass and accurate drift estimation, Charles landed us very near our old camp site at Wadi Halfa shortly before midday. I could not return to Baker with him, since he intended to take back a full load of fuel as well as the vital tool, so I visited the Commissioner with my tail between my legs and asked if another and better guide, complete with his own vehicle, was available to go south in search of our Land-Rovers. He said there was a man named Tawfiq, whose knowledge of the southern deserts was unequalled and whose genius at repairing anything wrong with a Land-Rover was positively inspired. He was also without a doubt the most expensive guide in the Nubian desert, and for the Akasha run during the time of the winds, he would charge a minimum of twenty guineas regardless of whether he reached Akasha or not. Tawfiq was a man of few words and no humour, but he made up for this by extreme efficiency at his job. Within an hour of his agreeing to take me south, we were off with spare petrol and oil next to a large box of spares and tools in the back of his ancient Land-Rover. A leather bag carrying well over a gallon of cool water hung from the side of the bonnet within my reach and a packet of biscuits and cheese lay on the shelf in front of me.

Tawfiq seemed to know exactly where he was whether the dust clouds closed in on us or not. His gear changes sometimes neatly anticipated steep unseen gradients and his direction finding, though he had neither stars nor moon to help him for all had become inky black soon after dusk, was faultless and according to my compass never veered far from south-south-east. Soon after midnight, he indicated that Sumna lay to our west, and that the others must pass the particular valley in which we were. No matter how far east they had strayed elsewhere, the nature of the country channelled all the valley floors past this area. We had not long to wait; I had dozed off and Tawfiq prodded me awake at four in the morning to indicate the twin sets of lights coming towards us from the south, jerking violently from time to time as though borne by a motor-boat in rough seas. Peter and Nick were driving at the time, Mike and the guide sleeping soundly, having both driven solidly for the earlier half of the night. They resembled ghosts with their large cracked lips and coating of white dust, and though obviously relieved to see us – for they were firmly convinced they were well off the route –they had little to say of their nightmare experience, wanting nothing but sleep away from the stinging blinding sand.

I gathered that Ali had at least proved his worth as a mechanic and, through his knowledge and a Heath Robinson lifting-gear, the burnt-out clutch plate had been changed in the worst of conditions in only six hours. Two trailer wheels and one vehicle tyre had punctured, and the electrical system on the old diesel had given up the ghost, rectified by Peter who declared it to be similar to that of a helicopter.

With Tawfiq leading, and Nick and I driving, we arrived back at Wadi Halfa not long after midday, and joined Charles and Anthony who were sound asleep on the floor in the commissioner's sitting-room. Ali retreated unabashed with his four guineas and Tawfiq received his larger sum, which he checked meticulously, without thanks but muttering his misgivings that such boys as Ali should be allowed to guide, let alone drive.

The commissioner's pretty wife woke us with coffee and fried fish for a homely supper which we ate on the floor before going back to sleep, rising only at dawn on the following day, the 10th, as the brilliant desert sunbeams threw disturbing patterns on our stubbly faces and sand wasps began their daily buzzing session in the commissioner's wattle roof. Each Nubian village has its 'oomdeh', or headman, and in Wadi Halfa the commissioner was acting in this local capacity as well as government representative. How many town councillors would open their arms and hearths to a group of dirty strangers keeping the oddest of hours, in our hospitable English society, I wondered, as the little room turned from pink to orange and the two children argued merrily next door.

Charles confirmed that both hovercraft were now back on the Halfa beach, though he wasn't too sure of the exact location of Baker since he had finally brought the latter back by night with Anthony navigating and what he described as a permanent broadside of three-foot waves. I felt this must be a well-stretched exaggeration for everything seems larger and more fearful in the dark, but the winds had indeed howled fiercely that night and I could imagine the feelings inspired by such a nocturnal crossing. When Charles had returned earlier to Baker and Anthony with the fuel and missing tool, he had done so in a locally-hired fishing smack leaving Burton at Wadi Halfa, since Anthony could not be expected to drive the craft for the first time in such conditions. The piston head had been replaced by torchlight, and they decided to leave at once since they felt the road-party might well have returned by then and be organising a search-party. Anthony was only too pleased to be leaving, since his night alone on that distant beach had been disturbed by strange sounds and noises as of creatures leaving the lake and ascending the beach. When he awoke there were three wizened horny lizards not unlike alligators and a good four feet in length. They eyed him as he extricated himself from his sleeping bag but didn't follow as he made hastily for the high ground. Only after they had slithered back into the water, as the sun rose, did Anthony realise their photographic qualities, as is usually the way when extraordinary happenings come the way of a cameraman unexpectedly.

Soon after Anthony had spotted the distant lights of Wadi Halfa on the final return voyage, one of the drive engines was swamped and gave out. Chaos ensued, and a darkened 'tunnel of horrors' must have been a picnic compared with the next few minutes. With only one drive engine in action and running at full revs, the whole machine cavorted madly of a sudden and began a series of giddy circles. The radio, the cameras, and all the other bits and pieces in the cockpit, flew across and entangled themselves with the controls. Having decided what had caused the sudden disaster, Charles managed to find the control panel and switch off first the functioning drive engine and then the lift motor. The wind still rushed and the waves rocked the little craft, but the moment of panic was over and it was soon apparent that the wind, coming from the western deserts, would eventually drift the Hawk to the Wadi Halfa side of the lake. The owner of the fishing smack had meanwhile alerted the commissioner and some twenty members of the Northern Frontier police were ranging the shore with torches having seen the Hawk's green navigation-light. Willing hands pulled the craft into the shore for the men had waded out into the cold waters as Charles flashed his torch.

There was a train leaving for Khartoum the following day which should still get us there in good time to prepare for the demonstration. Sayyid Moyadeen, our customs friend, managed to order us a couple of Sudan's rare open rail-wagons from Atbara which would apparently accommodate all our equipment with ease and little additional expense, so we worked throughout the day repairing the damage sustained during the winds by both hovercraft and Land-Rovers. Aided by the brawny police, Burton was retrieved from the cove to which it had floated the night before, and with much Dampstart and cleaning, started and hovered over the soft beaches into the Police Station yard where we lifted it onto a platform of jerrycans to change the skirt, for the seams had been badly weakened during the storm.

Mike and Anthony visited the site of the old Wadi Halfa Temple ruins with Mr. Moyadeen and on the way back arranged for a football team from another part of Wadi Halfa to come that night to our camp site with their drums and best singers. We prepared a log fire and Peter unearthed a couple of bottles of Glenfiddich. Mike was filtering petrol into a tin cooker affair of ours when the breeze changed and a thud of exploding ignition was the first warning of anything wrong.

Mike screamed and ran blindly from side to side, pawing himself in agony as a ball of flames enveloped him from knees to hair. It was so unexpected and sudden, there was a nightmarish period of stunned inactivity before we ran to him, rolling him in the flickering orange sand and heaping handfuls of it onto his face and hands. His hands were worst affected being soaked in fuel and fresh spurts of flame came from them when all seemed to have been extinguished. He was no longer screaming, but lay moaning, looking at the pitiful layers of blistered skin hanging in shrouds from his arms, lower stomach and thighs. Raw and bleeding flesh indicated the places where our ministrations with the smothering sand had been too violent.

I gave him a morphine jab and paraffin gauze dressings loosely applied but the sand was filthy and quite apart from the dreadful and steadily mounting pain, the danger from infection was extreme. There was a local hospital and we took him there, to a bed with used linen and a mosquito net to keep the flies away. Fortunately he could lie without pain on his undamaged back so long as he kept his lacerated arms and neck from touching anything. A doctor came within two hours and did his best to swab the gritty sand from the wounds before coating Mike in purple gentian violet. He mentioned twenty-five per cent burns without much air of certainty, but seemed sure that the patient would survive, which was the main thing.

Later the Nubian football team came, whilst Mike slept after more morphine, and wild Nubian songs accompanied the rhythmic tap of their goatskin drums far into the night. Their white djellabia robes flowing in the fitful gusts, they danced a strange version of the foxtrot with hands clapping in unison and grinning faces jerking puppet-like to emphasise the beat. The drummers squatted on Burton, feet drumming on the fibreglass hull, feet as black as the gleaming new hover skirt.

I have never met a more genuine and attractive people than the Nubians at home in their inhospitable deserts, and as we

119

left on the old steel puffing monster next day, I was not surprised to see the commissioner, Shell representative, police chief and customs officer, as well as the entire football team and fishing fleet owners, all turn up to wave us off with Allah's blessing.

# CHAPTER 8

∞

## *The Naked and the New*

'Tulip, tulip in Amsterdam . . .' was the rattling tune repeated by
our metal monster hauling its ancient coaches south to Abu
Hamed and Atbara, past Station Number Six where there is
water, and though there is virtually nothing else, what does that
matter when you see endless parched desert whichever way you
look and know that armies of proud men have died of thirst
whilst trying to reach this point.

Hot choking clouds of dust poured through the carriage
windows, mixed with specks of soot. We closed the windows,
only to saturate the wooden seats with our running sweat in
minutes. Better the dirt than a two-day sauna bath, so we opened
the windows again and suffered the lesser of two evils. But poor
Mike, swathed in purple bandages and wanting only to sleep to
forget his searing pains, could not afford to get dirt in his wounds
and we kept his window closed. He sweated horribly and the
salt ran down his burnt neck. I felt helpless listening to his
groans, and fed him bananas, aiming carefully at his mouth as
the train swerved madly, spitefully.

The word must have got around amongst the surly crew in
their hot and high-collared Sudan Rail coats; some English
milords were aboard having hired a first-class cabin and two
complete open rolling-stock for their amazing motor-boats. Our
arrival and the subsequent confirmation that we were, if milords
at all, of the new wave of scruffy non-tipping type, served only
to make these old black Jeeves's yet surlier and our carriage-
steward locked himself into his cabin determined to avoid us.

121

He had obviously met up with young Europeans before, and having been accustomed to the finery and generosity of the Edwardians, in the days when the Sudan was a second home to so many Englishmen, nothing pained him and his kind more than to have to react to the orders of the strange and mannerless youngsters that England now seemed to be producing by the score.

Our ancient friends, Alan and Jane, had travelled by this train almost a week before us. As they left the lake steamer at Wadi Halfa, Peter had noticed they had neither food nor water; he filled a bag with Horlicks rations and fruit and gave them a plastic water-holder. How they intended reaching Ethiopia, let alone their hazardous goal of tramping to Addis Ababa, without such basic necessities as water containers was mystifying and Peter had felt pangs of foreboding as he watched the old couple leave the barge waving their thanks.

A student of immense proportions and thick spectacles, which he was forever wiping clear of dust, was studying pamphlets in our cabin, his large fawnlike eyes rising from the print from time to time to inspect us.

Everything about Sudan Rail needs modernising and repair, but one can say that about many things in this beautiful land. Red tape and official fear of change are as much a hindrance to improvement as is lack of funds and there is the Government's false idea of fostering the country's prestige internationally. They were soon to get a number of Russian tanks to give the impression of armoured might to anyone who might care to notice. But what good would these be? There are very few motorable roads in the whole country, and only one or two stretches of surfaced tarmac. These would be the only routes firm enough to support tank movement, and how long before the grinding metal tank-tracks tear up even these and turn them into perennial quagmire like every other road in the country?

My thoughts were interrupted by our travelling-companion, "You must excuse me, I have not even introduced myself, and you will think we Sudanese have no manners. Mohamed Sadiq, I am very pleased to meet you. I have read of your journey and indeed hope to attend your hoverboat show in the city this week." In excellent English he went on to tell us of a British Army group who a year before had made their way across the Libyan deserts by way of Kufra intending to finish their journey in Khartoum. They never arrived. The press were kind about their abortive efforts but it helped to confirm the image the people seem to have these days of a withered and toothless British lion. Many of them remembered the time when no Englishman would think of turning back; when his words meant something for they were backed by confidence and, if necessary, action. Such a journey as ours, said Mohamed, could only do good between our countries. Sudan's leaders, when they could take their minds momentarily from political feuds, were concentrating on the vital question of trade as never before.

"You feel there is a market for hovercraft in the Sudan, then?" asked Charles. Mohamed said there had never been a hovercraft, nor to his knowledge a hovercraft agent, in the country. His country's main problem, the great hindrance to all ambitious improvement-schemes, was the almost complete lack of reliable communications. The Sudan is a country of 967,500 square miles, which is equivalent to say, Italy, France, Belgium, Spain, Portugal, Scandinavia and the United Kingdom lumped together, but less road or rail than any one of these countries.

To clarify their clumsy immensity still further, their most obvious line of communication, the Nile, is the longest river in the world but in fact only navigable in fairly useless stretches and it spends seven months of the year rendering nearly all Sudanese tracks within 100 miles of it flooded and unusable. The Sudan shares more common borders than any other country in the world: with Libya, the U.A.R., Saudi Arabia, Chad, Ethiopia, Kenya, Uganda, Congo and the Central African Republic. What a chance for easy trade, one might think, but swamps, deserts and jungles vie with wars and ignorance to make an empty dream of a potential trade Utopia.

Anything which, like our hovercraft, seems to offer a possible answer to the travel problems will always arouse a lot of interest in high places in Khartoum. Mohamed assured us there would be an enormous audience at the demonstration, but warned us not to be too encouraged by a spate of initial enquiries. Sudanese businessmen take a long time to make up their minds and we would need to establish a reliable agent who would have to work hard and patiently if we were to get any sales results. The British Hovercraft Corporation had had an agent there for some time, but it seemed he was an Italian, with conflicting interests in selling hydrofoil from Milan.

"God's blessing be with you," exclaimed Mohamed. "I gather you will be carrying on through the south. You will be the first foreigners to drive through the south for a very long time; indeed, I am amazed you have received permission at all."

We learnt a lot about the attitudes, problems and philosophies of the people of Khartoum from the friendly Mohamed. He had a genuine and consuming desire for the improvement of his country, which had nothing to do with politics and seemed a good sign of the way students are thinking at Khartoum University, the country's main seat of learning.

We stopped at Berber, a grotty, unstriking town and bought some fizzy applejuice and lumps of crushed dates. This was the scene of General Kitchener's most unworthy hour, where, after the battle of Atbara, which preceded the Khalifa's great defeat at Omdurman, Kitchener's highland warriors and Anglo-Egyptian troops held a victory parade in Berber. While their valiant general watched from his imperial white charger, the leading emir of the routed black masses was led, bleeding and badly burnt, to run the gauntlet of the troops. Tight metal bonds gripped his wrists and ankles, and threatened to throttle his straining throat. Proud and young, with noble blood, he could hardly have expected such treatment from his jeering British captors. Rape and murder were to follow, and the historians who dwell heavily and solely on the Mahdist atrocities would do well to eat dates on Berber station's dusty platforms and listen to any Sudanese student recount the tales of Anglo-Egyptian suppression in those cruel times. There were wrongs on both sides as in every war. Our young friend was quite open and friendly and indeed seemed to admire Kitchener's driving ambition, which allowed no sentiment to interfere with his aims nor the intermittent barbarity of some of his troops.

Perhaps Kitchener had long nursed thoughts of vengeance for

the gory day of defeat fifteen years earlier, when 10,000 troops under Colonel Hicks of the British Egyptian Army had been killed, already half-dead with thirst, as they marched to eliminate the Mahdist threat whilst it still germinated. A threat which then grew into the dreadful years of Mahdist rule, and was only suffocated finally at Omdurman, by when the population of the Sudan had been reduced through massacre, starvation and disease from some ten to a mere three million inhabitants. Or of General Gordon's defeat at Khartoum, a nineteenth-century Suez débâcle, when Britain's war-machine struggled hopelessly in the indecisive grasp of another weak, wet Whitehall; defeat which, in its aftermath, revealed the inhuman bloodlust of the Mahdist fanatics. They mutilated thousands of unarmed inhabitants whilst Khartoum burnt and Gordon's head went its grisly way.

All this was less than a hundred years ago, but not too easy to picture as we passed, soon after Berber, through peaceful Atbara with its throngs of raucous street-urchins and gangling camels, purple-dyed backs marking them as bound for the slaughter house. Here the daily slave parades were once held; gleaming naked bodies of every hue and both sexes receiving the intimate inspections of the dealers and buyers, while onlookers cracked crude jokes as to their origins and probable destinations. Darwin produced many an interesting theory on various 'tool-using' animals that show human ingenuity in their manipulation of inanimate objects to achieve certain tasks, but he never got round to theorising on the animal-like subjugation of whole races of humans by others, along the principle of worker bees with the slave dealers as the queen bees.

The dealers obtained ivory for their slaves, and with the ivory they made fortunes. The ivory went to Europe where the rich made comely fans, billiard balls, and keys for their pianos, which pattered prettily in lush drawing-rooms. A far cry from the soulful drumbeat echoing along the banks of the distant Nile where the proud elephant shrilled his childlike death cry and fell to have his tusks drawn out; where countless black humans died in silent perplexity, not knowing why and never having seen a billiard ball or a piano.

The rail, which was pioneered by Kitchener's engineers and

cuts out the vast Nile loop with its ancient capital cities, Dongola and Merowe, joins the river again at Abu Hamed and follows it fairly closely all the way to Khartoum. The journey can take anything between thirty hours and two days depending on the temperament of the monstrous steam locomotives that make the trip. We were only some eight hours behind schedule when we pulled in thankfully at Khartoum's uninspiring central station, having had more than enough of Sudan Rail's well-advertised comforts, acidic tea, and perpetual atmosphere of dust, soot and sweat.

Two of us had spent the overnight section of the journey in the cabins of the Land-Rovers being rocked to and fro on the open wagons to which our vehicles were lashed. The train stopped at several little stations overnight and, however late it was, the entire population of each village seemed to be congregated in readiness along the railside—there being few actual raised platforms—and porters and onlookers swarmed aboard, as soon as it stopped, to exchange gossip with the passengers. The diesel Land-Rover had no door locks and the other vehicle's locks had already proved no obstacle to a determined looter, so rather than patrol the vehicles at every stop through the night, we decided to sleep inside them. Our faces were thus a sooty grey on arrival at Khartoum, as were the Hawks and even our fluttering Sudanese flags which had replaced the Egyptian ones soon after we left Aswan.

The national flag is green, blue and yellow, symbolising the forest, the Nile and the sands. It is the Nile which unites the forests and the sands, the south and the north, and the new breed of politicians and officials which Khartoum is producing and sending out to the far flung southern provinces stress the point of unity above all others. Neither the North nor the South could survive economically without the other, they maintain, and secession by the South is the country's most critical issue, as it has been ever since the British first began to unofficially encourage the idea. All the politicians including ex-Prime Minister Sir Khatim el Khalifa, to whom I spoke on the topic, thought that the present civil war was a direct result of a mistaken policy during the British rule.

126

## The Naked and the New

The northern Arabs, ruling from Khartoum, despise the Negroid tribes of the south, and the innate feeling of superiority —which is in no way disguised by many of the government officials sent to the South—has much to do with the Southern determination to gain complete autonomy and sever connections with the North. The common generalisation that the Muslim North is engaged in a religious persecution of the Southern Christians is not totally accurate since many of the tribes are pagan, having their own rain-making gods.

We had noticed in Egypt that, whereas photography of the government officials in their westernised clothing is approved, that of the local fellahin stripped to the waist or even dressed in flowing djellabias is not. No reason was given to us for this odd form of censorship, so we presumed it to have risen from the official desire to demonstrate progress and modernisation in all things. Nubia had been refreshingly free from any form of official interference, but in Khartoum we ran once again into an undercurrent of officious suspicion and needless red tape which to some extent hung over our heads till we left the Sudan.

Many of the tribesmen we came across in the Nileside marshlands went naked about their daily business, their women wearing only a totally inadequate strip of bark in many cases; a sort of missing link between Eve's leaf and the G-string. But a fascinating array of scars, cicatrices with bright dyes and ornaments as well as an assortment of pronounced artificial deformities made up for any lack of clothes. These were obviously fine, proud people who disliked the restriction of clothing and anyway had no reason to hide their usually magnificent physique. The authorities must have felt otherwise, for we were expressly forbidden to photograph even the semi-undressed, those with tribal markings, or women whose feminine attributes were at all apparent.

With the strictly veiled Muslim women of Muscat and flirtatious but shy 'slave' girls of Salalah in Dhofar, I had found considerable difficulty getting reasonable photographs, especially in the more public spots such as the markets and wells where they were easier to run to ground. But the menfolk, even the local religious leaders, or 'walis', always treated my photographic manoeuvres with amused contempt, or else ignored them. Not so in Southern Sudan. Twice we were threatened with the confiscation of all the cameras and the censoring of films. A thoroughly bad atmosphere with the local police always resulted when we were found attempting photographic forays without their presence in the form of some odious and usually bespectacled officer who would have been equally at home in Papa Doc's Haitian strongarm force.

I fear my reactions to the unmannered and unreasonable Sudan security police were unnecessarily impatient, and a bit more forebearance in our later dealing with them might well have eased their treatment of us, or at any rate relaxed their vigilance. But it was difficult to shrug off their boorishness after my earlier months with the easy going Omani authorities, who go out of their way to be understanding to the few European visitors.

An example of the Omani laissez-faire had occurred—some three months earlier in Dhofar during a routine patrol to the deserted but still fertile gardens of Umran in the hope of capturing a group of rebels reported to be active in the area. It was said they were in the habit of sending men down to the old plantation shortly before dawn to collect supplies of limes and coconuts.

I positioned a ring of machine-guns and mortars in the surrounding hills during the night, and soon after dawn the following day spotted four men moving through the palm groves below my position. Someone reported seeing rifles glinting as they walked, so we fired a warning burst in front of them. Since they then sprinted for the cover of a deep river bed, my mortars opened up and we closed in on the area. A painstaking search of the thickly-treed ground revealed an old man with a prize-winning white beard and a skinny child, neither of whom were likely to have been carrying rifles. They may or may not have been with or seen the original group of four, so I took them back to the intelligence officer in Salalah. Within an hour I was summoned back to the latter's office and instructed to take the 'captives' back to where I had found them without delay. The old man was apparently the uncle of the Sultan's wife and had

Dinka kraals. The larger, more comfortable 'biers' were often for the cattle.

The humped Dinka cattle sport murderously long horns.

Soldiers from the 'war zone' arrive at Bor on the steamer from Juba.

Baker after the collapse of a bridge in the forest of Bor.

objected strongly—once in the presence of the Intelligence Officer who could understand his toothless Arabic—to having his morning stroll interrupted by mortar bombs. I dropped him back at the gardens with profuse apologies at having ruffled his royal personage, and no more was said. As with everything in the Oman, it is the Will of Allah. Would that the Sudanese authorities come round to the same easy-going ways.

*I*

# CHAPTER 9

∞

## Land of the Blacks

Countless millions of termites chew away at tree roots and crumble the soil in the deep Abyssinian gorges, causing a rich alluvial deposit which the waters of the Blue Nile take with them in their roisterous descent through the Land of the Lion. Nasser's 'little darlings', these ants might well be termed, for without their masticating ministrations, there would be no Nile Delta. At Khartoum these waters mix with those of their brother the White Nile, giving him a shot in the arm when he most needs it, having narrowly missed strangulation by the Sudd swamps and stagnation in the long stretches of low land south of the city. The sluggish White has already travelled two thousand eventful miles by the time it arrives here, and has another two thousand or so to go when it meets the Blue. Together they then run on through dry deserts, suffering the daily evaporation without further aid, for no other tributary joins them other than the Atbara which spends much of the year dry.

All Egyptian eyes turn then to Khartoum from where their lifeblood flows, to the country which their ancestors named Sudan—land of the Blacks.

Our train puffed with an air of finality over Omdurman rail-bridge, beneath which the two powerful rivers mingle and unite. The two colours are quite easily discernible, by no means white or even blue; rather a turgid green from the azure streams of the Abyssinian Highlands, and a murky khaki sieved through the southern swamps.

The British Military Attaché met us at the station and had

poor Mike driven straight off to Harper's Nursing Home, which is where the British diplomats and their families sleep off their stomach troubles and occasional attacks of malaria and jaundice. Clean sheets and a cooling fan, European cigarettes and cold drinks, Mike began to feel vaguely human again even though he didn't look it.

The Attaché very kindly opened his doors to us on learning that we had no other quarters arranged, and we ate like kings throughout our stay in Khartoum. He explained that the arrangements for the demonstration were all in the capable hands of one Brigadier Hussein Ali Karrar, an independent import agent of considerable initiative who was a retired Military Governor of the Blue Nile Province and during the Military Regime had been a member of the all-powerful Supreme Court, a body of three chief ministers who form a sort of cabinet to support or veto the President and Prime Minister. Since many of those in positions of power in the Army had only got where they were through the friendship and earlier guidance of Brigadier Karrar, who had long presided at the Army Staff College, he was a valuable friend and we would undoubtedly have got no farther than Khartoum had it not been for his aid in the corridors of power. We met him the following morning and he discussed our problems.

The 'haboob' season was not far off when Khartoum suffers badly from fine dust clouds which come in from the deserts that more or less surround the city. It becomes impossible to see your own hand stretched out in front of your eyes when the wind comes, even though it's noon on an otherwise cloudless day, and there's yet to be the door or window designed which will keep the dust out. Housewives go mad sweeping and carpet-beating and many store everything of value away in boxes while the haboob lasts. It's far worse than the thickest of Kent fogs.

"A lot depends on the reliable performance of your craft tomorrow," said the Brigadier. He explained that a number of people would be watching us who could directly affect our movements once we had left Khartoum for the South. The rebels had been getting a lot of external support of late and a renewed flare-up of violence in the areas we would be going through was very much on the cards. No-one could tell, but it added a considerable risk to our presence in the south; not a risk which the authorities would necessarily want to take.

"But all that was fixed and in writing months ago," I protested, "and they can't change their minds now that we've got here, surely?" It was really more a question than a statement, for it struck me that the brigadier knew far more than he cared to let on for fear of disappointing us.

He sighed and said the sooner we realised that things in the South just didn't happen according to the normal rules and practices, the sooner we would be prepared to accept the number of disappointments we were almost bound to receive, especially if in a hurry. Our sense of urgency would not be understood and would get us nowhere. Things would probably work out all right if all went well at the demonstration and he could get a word in the right ears at the right moment. He had heard that I knew their ex-Prime Minister, Sir Khatim, which should be a help since he was then in Khartoum on holiday from London. He would almost certainly be going to a party one of the brigadier's sons-in-law was holding that night. I was to go to the party with the brigadier and he would see what could be arranged. Meanwhile, he would take us round to a number of officials and we should get at least a few documents arranged to put us on an official footing. He felt that the Security Police would be the main obstacle to allowing us south of Kartoum, and to be fair, it was, after all, entirely their responsibility if anything should happen to us or should we later discredit the country with our films and articles.

The brigadier did not wish to discourage us, but even if we did get the expedition on an apparently official footing with Government support, there was still no assurance that we would not be turned back by any one of the regional authorities in the South. They inclined to be laws unto themselves and were as often as not quite out of touch with Khartoum, either through the wires going down during a local storm, or due to rebel wire-cutters.

I told the brigadier that as long as, with his help, we were allowed out of Khartoum, I felt sure any problems in the South would resolve themselves. The brigadier's car was a spacious

Volkswagen, but he had earlier owned Jaguars and a Rolls and explained in indignant tones that all car prices were prohibitive under the contemporary government, almost doubling U.K. prices. We drove along the river-bank hoping to find a suitable place to disembark the hovercraft the next morning. Tuti Island faces Khartoum's residential bank of the Blue Nile where the more influential people live and Gordon's Palace lies in a bed of stunning colour, for the extensive gardens are still well looked after. Kitchener's Avenue runs along the river embankment shaded by cool green sycamore and haraz trees, home of the soft cooing turtle-doves who induce pleasant drowsiness in the politicians whose offices and Ministries are centred around the Palace.

The banks were steep and high wherever we looked. No place for Burton to enter the water, even after we had followed the richly foliaged river-bank for over a mile, so we followed the road over the Omdurman Bridge and soon came to a spot with smoothly sloping beach. Camel-droppings in thick layers littered the area for here was their drinking-ground. It struck me that Charles would be smelling pleasantly of camel dung on his introduction to the President the next day for the Hawk has an evil habit of blowing any loose substance from beneath its skirt into a fine spray all round, and if, as in hot weather, the doors are left open, then also inside the cockpit. Once the machine has lifted itself off the ground, the spray ceases, but by then the driver is covered in sand, mud, grass, or as in this case, fresh camel dung.

Having established a reasonable start point, we returned for a series of interviews with the various ministers concerned with our journey. First the brigadier showed us the rest of Omdurman, now an uninteresting place much like most Middle East towns slowly becoming suffused with messy blotches of a westernised character, but a place where the past still seems to cling. The restless souls who suffered shame and agony in Omdurman not so long ago never seem far below the surface, despite the urban peace and cheerful appearance of the people. Sit by the river for a while when the sun is falling behind the low roofs and the devout unroll their prayer mats, a strange oppression strangles the mind; it is not a happy place, not a place where I would choose to unroll my sleeping bag for the night, even if the mosquitoes didn't look, and sound, like wasps.

When the Mahdi died, probably through over indulgence in food and women, he was buried in a richly-constructed tomb that soon became a Muslim shrine. It was thought to be a holier place even than Mecca and pilgrims travelled from all over the world to visit Omdurman. It was also a major slave and ivory market.

Less than a century ago it was a common spectacle to see more than a hundred naked slaves chained to each other in long lines and staked to the bank. Those who had not angered their masters would have chains sufficiently long to allow them to drink from the river. Sanitary arrangements were not needed and a handful of durra flour shortly before the evening market made them a little livelier, so that their appearance with the added bonus of a healthy sheen from well-applied coconut oil was as attractive as possible to the buyers. Young boys and girls were in high demand and underwent careful inspections; a coin might be thrown into the mud for them to fetch and show their grace of movement in doing so—Crufts with a difference. It was the Arabs who introduced homosexuality amongst the Africans and the desirability of young eunuchs to the slave market and the growing trade of castration without killing the victim was flourishing, though more often than not the mutilation carried out in the mud, with the patient still attached to his chained fellows, proved fatal.

Slaving dhows carrying captives from the Khartoum markets and elsewhere still sailed from Zanzibar and ports along the Red Sea coast as late as 1870 and very few were intercepted by the European men-of-war. The south-westerly monsoon winds began in June, and speeded the ships of sin on their way to the Pirate Coast of Trucial Oman, blowing themselves out only in the latitudes of the frankincense coast of Dhofar. These monsoons cover the mountains of Dhofar for four months of the year during which the thick rain-clouds cause a permanent drizzle that turns the region into a lush green paradise quite unique in Arabia and not unlike southern Wales in spring.

On our way back to Khartoum, we stopped at the central post office and stuck the cheapest version of the national stamp onto 500 of the White Nile Hovercraft Expedition envelopes. The postal workers thought this a great innovation; seven of them were soon licking busily and the manager raised no objection to postmarking the lot. The earlier sets of five hundred had been completed at Alexandria, Aswan and Wadi Halfa, and since the four fairly large boxes containing them took up a lot of valuable room in the Land-Rovers, I decided to post them back to the dealer. The diplomatic bag seemed as safe a way as any but in fact turned out to be the slowest, for the boxes eventually turned up at the irate London dealers some four months later, having spent a month in Mombasa and then sailed round the Cape.

Shell-Sudan has its headquarters beneath the British Embassy and the marketing manager was most helpful. He felt there would be no problem in the South, for even where garages are few and far between, there are nearly always government rest-houses with their own fuel supplies or passing military convoys with a taste for English cigarettes. He reckoned we would need to plan for a maximum of two hundred miles without refuelling facilities. This would be no problem since we could carry a total of ninety gallons when all the cans were full. As we progressed south and, without noticing it, the altitude increased, the hovercraft required higher octane fuel, so that on reaching Malakal, we obtained Avgas aviation fuel from the Shell agent at the local airstrip. None of the garages we visited even in the most far-flung spots objected to giving us credit, a fact for which we were particularly thankful, having no ready cash, and driving as we did for over seven hundred miles without passing a bank.

I posted off a report on the progress we had made over the last two weeks to the *Daily Telegraph,* who were meant to be getting a report weekly, though I found this to be impossible owing to the lack of postal facilities along much of the route. Of the three reports I sent from the Sudan, two never arrived nor did the enclosed photographic negatives, whether because of some unsuspected censor or through the unreliability of the postal services, I never found out. But the Sudanese Press Attaché in London must have had word of our passage for our Military Attaché in Khartoum gave me a recent copy of the *Daily Telegraph* which stated that our 'expedition was doing much to improve the friendship and goodwill between Britain and the peoples of Egypt and the Sudan'. This was heartening and partially offset the fact that we didn't seem to have sold any of the equipment yet, let alone a hovercraft.

The brigadier stopped by a small neat house not far from the Shell Sudan Centre which turned out to be the Ministry of Communication's Tourist Department. The director was a friend of the brigadier's and had heard of our problems. His office smelled pleasantly of tobacco and well-polished leather. The blinds were down and soft lighting glinted off a hundred objects of interest on the spacious shelving all round the room. Mr. Achmed Abu Bakr loved his country and his job. Few people can have travelled as extensively as he within the Sudan, and his office contained a rare collection of antiques, geological specimens, handicrafts and paintings from every corner of the vast country. He had spent many weeks on safari in the south-east with both rifle and cameras, and showed us some amazing sequences of the little-known tribes of the Karamajong area north of Uganda with such evocative names as the Didinga, Topotha, and Longarim. The Director waxed strong on his favourite subject, explaining that . . . for the American family wanting a fortnight's 'luxury safari' with a good look at a cross section of Africa's beasts, and an air-conditioned tent with cocktail cabinet to retire to when the sun gets hot, Kenya and Uganda would take a lot of beating. But for the keen hunter of the wild and untamed lion, rhino, rogue elephant or any other genuine trophy, the Sudan is unequalled. He said there are many areas, particularly in the south-east where every imaginable type of game roams with little fear of the hunter, simply through the remoteness and the lack of communications. There are animals to be hunted and photographed there which can be found nowhere else: the giant eland, the bongo, white-eared cobs and yellow-backed duikers, even the Nile lechwe which goes under the homely name of Mrs. Grey.

After an interesting hour of slides and hunting stories, whilst being plied with iced coffee, sherbet and Turkish cigarettes, we received the director's official blessing for the expedition and what was, so we thought, even more important, a document giving us permission to take still and ciné films in the south, with the sole proviso that we showed them to a representative of the Sudanese Government in London before releasing any of them for public viewing.

London lunch-hours are mere coffee breaks compared with the midday siestas enjoyed by most Khartoum businessmen, so the brigadier took his leave of the Tourist Director and flung his Volkswagen round the somnulent city, back to the drowsy shade of the phoenix palms by the Palace. The guards saluted, slapping bayonetted automatics in a fair attempt at unison; the brigadier was known to all, but I fingered my oily jeans and smoothed them subconsciously. This was, after all, the Houses of Commons and Lords rolled up into one, and we were bound for the office of the Minister of the Interior, officially prime mover of the Security Police.

I wasn't too sure, after a blurred introduction whether or not we were speaking to the Minister himself or his First Secretary. This was one Sayyid Zeeyada, a severe-looking individual with thick shaded spectacles which confused the direction of his glance in a disturbing manner. It was painfully apparent that life would take an immediate turn for the better for Mr. Zeeyada as soon as he managed to get the Hovercraft Expedition out of his hair. He made no bones about this, and feeling put out, I assured him we were only too keen to get going and that as soon as he or his minions allowed us the necessary documents and the vital permit to motor through the South, he would be rid of us. The brigadier put this to him in Arabic in subtler, more delicate tones and added that the British Embassy would vouch for our character and status even if they weren't actually taking any responsibility for the expedition.

The tinted spectacles gleamed ambiguously and our fate hung presumably in balance. I smiled at the man and knocked my iced Coca Cola over onto what might once have been one of General Gordon's carpets. An orderly swooped to replace the glass and mop up the stain. His Nibs said he would consult his associates—not superiors—and rose to inform us that his lunch-hour was nigh. I didn't see him again but the all-important papers did arrive later that day, together with the promise of an escort from Kosti, some thirty miles south to Khartoum, all the way to the Ugandan border. It wasn't clear what this escort would consist of, but the brigadier felt it would be provided by the police as far as Malakal which was roughly at the northern edge of the swamp areas, and thereafter by the Army who were active throughout the South.

Mike Broome was sitting up taking a decided interest in life when we visited him that afternoon with iced beer and a ticket to London for the following morning. His hands would obviously require extensive skin grafts and infection had set in below the blisters which was not surprising. He left the next morning during the demonstration and gave a stirring description of the tender attentions of the air hostess when next I saw him weeks later. It was extremely sad to see him go, for he was permanently cheerful and optimistic; rare qualities in a good photographer, particularly when conditions are anything but favourable. His skill and imagination would have had plenty of scope during our route up the White Nile, and I later felt very inadequate on many occasions trying to capture on celluloid the amazing scenes, the wonderful colours and moods in that strange world of the swamp tribes.

There were crowds of Europeans and Khartoumers gathered round Burton and Baker, both parked outside the home of the Military Attaché. Every now and again a warning grunt from inside one of the craft and a bucketful of dirty water would cascade from the cockpit onto the pavement, splashing white shirts but not in the least detracting from the determined curiosity of the onlookers. Charles had decided to give both craft a spring clean for the benefit of the President.

Amongst the throng were three gaily-coloured Daf motor-cars in the middle of the road. Their roof-racks were packed with obvious expertise and at a glance contained everything a trans-world motorist might need were he expecting no resupplies for six months. A placard on the bumper of each Daf proclaimed them to be Stichting Operation Giraffe. The driver of one approached us, having been unable to get near Charles in safety. They were a Dutch expedition he said—after satisfying his curiosity as to our own identity—and were intending to take their three little automatic cars right round the entire coast of Africa, passing through over forty different countries en route. The journey was the idea of twin brothers, Loek and Jim Vermeulen, with the help of the Dutch Charity Organisation, Stichting. They were incredibly well organised and I felt ashamed of the amorphous conglomeration of equipment sticking out from beneath our own bulging Land-Rover canopies. Their journey would take them a year or so and would require some twenty-three thousand litres of petrol. They would be producing a book with details of road conditions, petrol, water and accommodation facilities available on the roads of Africa.

"We have already found ourselves wishing we had Land-Rovers on several occasions," said Luis Ludoph, the navigator of the group. "Four-wheel drive is a must in this country, but of course our Dafs are very light and easy to push when bogged. There is a stretch in the Spanish Sahara where we will reckon to progress at a rate of about eight hundred yards in two days. It is so hot there that it would be quite possible to fry an egg on the floor of the car, if it weren't for our polyethylene heat insulation."

I would have wagered a considerable sum at Ladbroke's that the Dafs would never survive the awesome task they had been set. They might have been light but they were heavily laden and pushing cars out of sand, floods and bogs through much of Africa is a wearying proposition. Most tracks in Africa have deep ruts which make high road-clearance a must, and the Dafs' small wheels are not much larger than those of a Morris mini. Also they had failed to get permits to enter the South.

That evening whilst the others explored the night haunts of the teenage Khartoumers, I accompanied the brigadier to his son-in-law's party, held in the most salubrious part of the town where expensive European cars lined the dust 'pavements' like so many symbols of success; political success probably, since nearly all the guests—an international gaggle—were diplomats, a colourful mixture of ambassadors and government officials with their wives or series of wives. The latter were dressed to kill, long evening-dresses of every conceivable pattern and cut, except for the plunging neckline, conspicuous by its absence.

The British Ambassador, Sir Robert Fowler, looked distinguished, with an intellectual air that went well with bald head and immaculate suit. He had long been expecting our arrival, and greeted me without so much as a glance of disapproval at my shoddy appearance (outsize Khartoum supermarket slacks and ill-fitting tropical shirt bought hastily for the occasion). If all our diplomats were as lacking in social pomposity —understanding the difficulties of the traveller who finds himself in unexpectedly elevated social surroundings—we would indeed have the finest diplomatic corps in this difficult profession. Sir Khatim Al Khalifa was present and as friendly as he had been in London, though I noticed a definite reluctance on his part to discuss either past or present politics, especially with reference to the South. I put this down to a simple aversion to talking what was to him shop, outside the confines of his office. He said he hoped to attend the show the next day and see us all alive in London before too long.

The food was waiting in an elegant hall; a sight I shall undoubtedly remember in all its delectable detail whenever the pangs of hunger attack. Three sides of the long room were set with plate upon plate of scrumptious and exotic morsels on a background of thick white tablecloth, behind which moved a set of liveried caterers, though the mode was help-yourself. I had run out of people to talk to, and so began an hour's guzzle-in, which must have broken many records, both in quantity and variety, and which I would love to repeat, even though the consequences the following day were severe, since my stomach had gone without acclimatisation from the ridiculous to the sublime—no offence to Horlicks Iron Rations.

The feast had been washed down by a variety of wines, so I was grateful to be driven back by the brigadier though the breathalyser had happily not yet reached the Sudan. My attempt at silent entry without waking the Military Attaché ended in anguished minutes perched on his garden fence whilst his two little watchdogs snarled viciously from the lawn below, making noise enough to turn both the Mahdi and Gordon over in their graves had their bodies not been consigned by their respective enemies into the Nile and a Khartoum well. The poor brigadier was bitten by one of these dutiful hounds the following morning. It was definitely not his day, for I reversed one of the Land-Rovers at speed into his Volkswagen after tea at the British Ambassador's residence, whilst following the confident hand-directions of a liveried chauffeur.

The fourteenth was a public holiday and when we drove Burton round to Omdurman the whole town seemed to have turned out to catch a glimpse of the strange craft which local gossip had credited with the most amazing abilities: they could fly, swim, or drive on roads, all at unbelievable speeds, and the Government was to buy many dozens of them for some new and progressive scheme on the river. Would that the latter half of the rumour had been true.

Burton was left midst the camel dung and a swelling, excited crowd with Charles, as unflustered as ever, making his final preparations for what promised to be Khartoum's largest-ever commercial demonstration. Dampstart was sprayed carefully over every exposed electrical component—and liberally too, for the wind was gusting strongly and there would be much spray. All engines ticking over whilst rev counters with swinging needles confirmed their condition. A sudden cloud of choking camel dung, scattering startled onlookers and Burton was off, sliding with surging speed from the bank and away with a powerful wind astern.

We watched the white speck lose itself in the green distance where the great rivers meet and the bulk of Tuti Island obscures the wide loop which the Blue Nile follows before leaving Khartoum. We drove off through the thick holiday-traffic of Omdurman Bridge and its approach roads, part motorised, but largely bicycles and careless pedestrians, with half an hour to go before the President's arrival. Policemen waving white-gloved hands directed us to the spectators' area, and crossing beneath ropes into a cordoned-off part of the river bank directly in front of the Palace, we found Baker in a position of arrogance with shiny hoversnout tilted upwards. Around the craft Peter

141

had laid out the loaned equipment and a heap of assorted sales pamphlets. There had been a mild altercation between two members of the expedition the previous afternoon which had resulted in our magnificent water filter being broken over someone's head and so not available for the equipment exhibition; a pity since we found a real potential market for water filters in the Sudan.

A band was doing its duty somewhere and martial music blending with the motor-horns and eternal cooing of doves in the Phoenix palms. Sunlight came through the foliage in bright shafts wherein the rainbow dust danced and rippled over the heads of the throng, striking the rows of medals bouncing from proud khaki chests. The Army was well represented; the commander-in-chief had arrived with his retinue of staff officers and area commanders, and was accepting the attention of the press and film-men.

"No, the Army had no definite plans one way or the other regarding the purchase and use of hovercraft either in the South or anywhere else. The commander-in-chief is here to see the Sudan's first hovercraft demonstration—for no other reason."

And then as a slight, but noticeable hush fell over the audience below the palms, a Rolls-Royce of ancient vintage and regal purple sheen drew up smoothly by Baker's enclosure. A miniature national flag fluttered from its mid-bonnet pennant as Army and police saluted and a purple-clad chauffeur opened the door for the President. The three-man Parliament or Supreme Court appeared behind him and I shook all their hands. The loudspeaker I had been furnished with by a thoughtful brigadier whistled and reduced my tones to a moan, so I addressed the President and spectators without it, giving them a brief and sketchy description of the craft's functions and features, all of which was repeated as inaudibly by interpreter.

Nick signalled that Charles had arrived and sure enough a sigh from the crowd, now pressing to the embankment rails, indicated Burton's presence. The police cleared a space for the President who, being decidedly on the small side and, judging by the thick lenses of his spectacles, fairly short-sighted, had some difficulty in spotting Burton's whereabouts. The machine appeared to have gone wild—cavorting in a giddy succession of three sixty-degree skids directly beneath the steep bank from which we watched. For a second I felt sure Charles had lost control in the strong wind, then, not far from the bank itself, Burton veered round elegantly and with an audible surge of acceleration headed downstream and into the wind.

Peter was controlling Charles' movements through the Squad-pack radios, judging the mood of the crowd. Now Burton swung right across the broad river and side-slipped in the cross-wind. It was heading straight for the sandy shores of Tuti Island and nearing thirty knots. The President seemed alarmed—there would be an accident. But no, bucking like a spirited thoroughbred, the little white machine, accelerating still, left the water and roared over the undulating dunes between logs and other chance jetsam, sending up a sudden spray on reaching the water the far side of the island. A cheer of wonder and rapturous chattering between the spectators greeted this performance.

The wind was now behind Burton, and setting a straight course with virtually no drift, Charles sped upstream at a speed of which I had not thought the Hawks capable, even though the craft was of course carrying minimal weight . . . the hefty Charles and a radio.

For well over the intended half-hour, Charles kept Burton charging round the arena in fine style, and the crowd never failed to produce a deep Oooo-Ahhh each time the craft transferred from water to land without apparently noticing the difference. Even the least sophisticated Sudanese had become accustomed to cars and aeroplanes, but this was a new element —and one which they were quite at a loss to understand.

The commander-in-chief of the Sudan Army took the radio telephone from Peter and, speaking direct to Charles, had him take Burton in a series of tight loops around Tuti Island. He was fascinated by the way Burton took the beach in its stride, seeming to treat it merely as a bumpy extension of the Nile. But the day was hot and the sun reaching its zenith. Charles told Peter that, with the perpetually circular course and the strong west wind, he was having to keep all units at full throttle in order to maintain maximum speed and the little engines might well overheat if kept much longer at full pitch. The commander-in-chief and the other military and civilian potentates who took the telephone from him, were all eager to have a 'go' at radio-controlling the craft and would not listen to my apologetic mutterings. Charles was beginning to give unrepeatable replies into the Racall as the interminable and imperious directions reached him. He said he was losing precious pounds in sweat and that the cockpit was like a plate-glass greenhouse. This was very likely since Burton, unlike Hoverhawks which are produced specifically for hot climes, had no air-conditioning and both side doors were shut with fixed windows. The situation was beginning to look faintly tricky, for overheating during a demonstration—either of craft or pilot—is obviously not desirable. Fortunately a roar of full-throated cheering turned the attention of the officials who sprang to attention—Sayyid Ismael el Azhari, the President, was leaving. Before sinking back into the well-cushioned Rolls, he thanked us for the demonstration and wished us well on our continued journey through his country, saying that there was definitely a great future for hovercraft in the Sudan. Peter meanwhile tactfully removed the radio telephone from an official and gave a much relieved Charles the word to depart while the going was good—which he did and soon Burton was a distant blur on Tuti Island's long palm-fringed beach.

We shall never know whether or not we pleased the President and his officials with our hovercraft display, for only a few months after we left, a military coup overthrew the President and his regime, expressed a decidedly pro-communist policy line, and jailed a number of unsuspecting Englishmen for 'spying activities'.

It may have been this anti-British policy which later deterred the Sudanese from buying Hoverhawks. But whilst we were there, there were virtually no open signs of the impending troubles, though photography was discouraged even in the capital. The wife of our Military Attaché had been at Khartoum Airport the week previously and, about to take a harmless photo of Prince Philip arriving, was stopped by a security goon who became most unpleasant when she objected that he was after all her Prince and the background was a British plane.

Since the military coup d'etat tourists are now precluded from entering vast areas of the country, including most of the route we followed, but we had our papers and the President's approval so all seemed set for the final, longest and most important stretch of our journey. But as we basked in the glow of congratulations and a flood of enquiries for sales details of the Hawk, black thunder-clouds were gathering over the swamp-lands of the south, and the Dinka rain-makers cast bloodshot eyes to the dark scudding skies, their prophetic incantations telling the tribes to leave the river pastures; that the Giver of the Floods was impatient this year.

K

# CHAPTER 10

∞

## *Arrest in Malakal*

South of Khartoum, rolling grasslands pan away from the river on every side, dotted sparsely with acacia, thorn bush, and tamarisk. Dirt tracks meander between villages of thatched rondaaval huts which reflect a thin veneer of Khartoum's civilising influence. For many miles the occasional conspicuous white of a government building, the endless line of electricity posts which serve to emphasise the vastness of the land. There is little of interest or aesthetic pleasure in these parts, but the Jebel Aulia dam, some thirty miles south of the capital, afforded us a diversion, for the Hawks had to be loaded onto their trailers and taken round the dam and its immediate environs where the banks are stone-shod. Some way past the busy town of Ed Dueim, the river-banks shelved gently and the vehicle track came close to the water; a place where bedouin take their camels and flocks to drink their fill and drown their fleas. A good place for a camp and refuelling.

The day's heat lessened but slightly with the evening; a clammy heat putting us in a touchy, easily-irritated frame of mind which was aggravated yet further by the flying ants that seemed to settle on the eyelids whenever they could, and hosts of flies — large fat noisy ones, little gnat-like ones with a potent bite, and various intermediate shapes and sizes — all hellbent on discouraging tourists in the Nile Valley. I noticed that scratches and sores tended to suppurate and grow into swollen areas that hardly responded to antiseptic creams and penicillin. This was probably due to the humidity as much as the perpetual ministrations of the

146

flies. My finger, broken two months earlier in the Oman, was now badly poisoned, and various open sores on my feet, from wading in the river whilst tending to the Hawks, refused to heal. This made shoes painful to wear, though they were very necessary, for the whole area was covered in camel thorns—even where there were no thorn trees—and a camel thorn broken and embedded in the foot would cause severe blood poisoning.

Dusk arrived as we worked beneath one of the hovercraft, strengthening the skirt with pop rivets where floating logs had weakened the material. Empty jerrycans propped up the 900 pounds of fibreglass and metal. The Land-Rovers could provide sufficient light to work by after the sun had set, but we had to look after the batteries and fuel was low at the time. The hypnotic whine-hum of mosquitoes came with the dusk and made me wonder whether a bite leads the ear to the noise, already heard and acknowledged by the subconscious, for there is no single moment when one actually starts to hear them. Our legs stuck bare from beneath the craft and presented an enticing feeding-ground for the black and white striped brutes with their vicious needles.

The itching, not the fading light, decided us to stop work. Tools could stay where they lay for no tribesman would venture near the apparitions after dark. On its pedestal of jerrycans, Baker squatted brooding, a piebald toad with enormous eyes and gaping mouth.

The fire started well between some rocks, and yesterday's meat sizzled with onions and eggs. Peter lay writing his diary, finding doubtful inspiration in the play of flames; wondering perhaps how Mike had fared in the London hospital. Large skin grafts to his hands probably, as the infection had been deep, and the sand we had pressed so frantically to his burning skin alive with evil microbes—for the fishermen of Halfa have no lavatories and minute sand-flies spread the dirt over each particle of sand.

We would finish work on the skirt after dawn on the morrow and with luck both craft would be away soon after breakfast. Speed was vital, for the Military Attaché in Khartoum had warned us that the first rains were even now beginning in the far south. Soon all vehicle tracks within a hundred miles of the river would be waterlogged and painfully slow, and after a few days of heavy rain, impassable for the next seven months. This would affect the hovercraft, too, for all our refuelling points were by the river, and well off the main track; certainly not attainable once the grass prairies turned to marsh. Pessimistic thoughts lead nowhere, but sleep came slowly with the dank humidity and the frenetic riot of sound that battered the ears. Crickets clacked and scraped with fervour but were drowned in noise-density by the macabre night tones of their countless slimy neighbours. The endless reverberating croak of giant toads provided a background to the specialists in sound, Caprimulgus nightjars whose mellow churr is almost sensuous to the ear. Marsh-owls with quick resonant hoots swished past as the rustle of reeds touching in the wind rose and fell fitfully.

We reached Kosti late the next afternoon, the 17th, and noticed a marked increase in the floating water-hyacinth. The road party had already arrived and unloaded on a muddy spit several miles downstream from Kosti bridge. The Hawks charged into a thick bank of hyacinth, breaking through onto the spit, where both were refuelled. We decided against spending the night there as planned, for the locals had taken umbrage at what they considered to be our high-handed behaviour. When three or four hundred individuals crowd in avid curiosity onto a narrow mud spit, each trying to get nearer to the objects of interest than the next, it makes refuelling, servicing and generally manoeuvering hovercraft virtually impossible without a few words of friendly advice to the offenders to clear some space. These were rendered in my best and most beatific Arabic, and had not the slightest effect on the milling mass which appeared to be increasing in size by the minute; they simply repeated my phrase in chorus, beating time on each others' bare backs.

It was quite impossible to reach the vehicles at the other end of the spit to get the necessary tools and make sure that the Land-Rovers were not completely denuded of equipment by the inevitable light-fingered experts. Peter, on the far side of the mob, saw our plight and made a timely appearance with a vanload of the local police. Little rhino-hide whips cracked effectively and the spit was cleared in a trice. The locals evidently knew all about rhino skin. But they did not disperse, just hung about in groups and the wide smiles were gone.

The impetus of the hovercraft had carried them through the hyacinth barrier onto the spit, but the mauve-tinged weed which had sprung up buoyantly behind them became a formidable obstacle again over which the Hawks could only go at near maximum speed. This they failed to obtain in the small space available although, once the police had disposed of the onlookers, we used the entire length of the spit as a runway—Burton surging off in a shower of spattered mud. Unfortunately the speed gained along the spit was only sufficient to take Burton some twenty feet into the hyacinth, where it became ensnared by the thick dragging weed. Wading out into the evil mud, fighting a way through the glutinous slime and offending reeds, Nick and I reached Burton, which still hovered hopelessly like a duck with no legs, succeeding only in blackening our faces and blinding us.

Half an hour with the aid of a tow rope had Burton back on the spit, and then an interminable struggle with the hyacinth to clear a temporary freeway. Little islands of green kept breaking from the main mass and floating back from whence we had pushed them. Eventually a five-foot gap through the vegetation rewarded our efforts. Charles and Peter drove hell-for-leather down the ramp, and we watched—up to our necks in the slime— as the Hawks made the open river and soon disappeared in the direction of the bridge.

The hyacinth, which we grew to hate, is some six inches high, a pinkish bloom on a bed of fat green leaves. The bulbous stalk and roots, which are buoyant, are blown hither and thither by the wind, haphazardly joining together in floating islands. Since there were nearly always passages between these obstacles, the Hawks' only real problem was finding a clear area through which to enter the water after a halt. Even this handicap would have been avoided had we used 'frill skirts', similar to our own except for a fringed extension all the way round which serves to allow obstacles of a certain height under the craft without damage to the skirt or disturbing the air cushion.

Nick and I, black as the disgruntled spectators, climbed—smelling of putrefaction—into the Land-Rovers, and thankfully left the town behind us. We followed the rough track south to where it meets the rail. Road and rail run parallel for half a mile and then together cross the British-made metal bridge; rail in the centre and an eight-foot wide passage for motors either side. Both trailers exceeded this width and we jammed the walled approach road as we pondered the problem.

Just as we decided our best chance lay in manhandling the trailers over the rails, a policeman arrived to discourage the idea. It was definitely forbidden and, judging by his urgent gesticulations, a train was due any minute—or at least any day—now. The Land-Rovers quite obviously would not help, nor would we have any trouble getting them over, so having reversed our little convoy back down the walled stretch, the trailers were detached. The crossing was not to be laughed at even in the trailer-less Land-Rovers, for the planking was loose and metal walls either side sprouted nuts from the roughly aligned girders.

I spotted the gleam of fibreglass from Burton or Baker and the curling blue smoke of a wood fire on the marshy bank farther upstream. So much for our other half; but they would have to keep the evening brew warm for though our stomachs yearned, the trailers must come first. We pushed the lighter one up the approach road to the point where the metal walls closed in and it just would not fit any further. A grocery lorry—an aged Commer truck—arrived with a squeal of brake-lining. The driver's initial reaction to the blockage of his evening run over the bridge was outrage, indignant pumping of his three-toned horn, accompanied by a string of Sudanese oaths and violent consultation with the thirty or forty white-robed human sardines clinging to his load.

With realisation that the obstacle was of English manufacture, the din increased but the outrage gave way to curiosity. Never before had two Englishmen—pocket-size Union Jacks were still stuck to our rear bumpers—been seen on Kosti bridge in so strange a situation; nor was it apparent how they had managed to get so large a trailer, without visible means of towing, into such a position. Our unaided efforts at up-ending the trailer in a futile attempt at manhandling it between the narrow walls, had succeeded only in wedging it firmly between them.

At first it appeared that the driver and his many companions would help, for they took hold of the trailer and manoeuvred it with ease. But our hopes were shortlived for, with a series of surprisingly co-ordinated heaves, they moved it back to its earlier position and propped it on its side against the fence out of their way. Without acknowledging our rather doubtful thanks, they remounted and were off, covering us with dust and dourra flour —which formed a picturesque mixture with the undercoat of Nile mud.

A succession of Commer lorries now came past us; it was quite hair-raising to watch the turbanned drivers propelling their heavily laden lorries, seemingly tailor-made for Kosti bridge, between the metal walls. With not much more than a finger's breadth either side and wheels bouncing on the loose planks, they were over in a jiffy, ignoring the occasional screech of metal on metal. They were transformed men at the wheel, the twenty-four-hour daily siesta of their grounded brethren forgotten as soon as accelerator and horn warmed the blood.

Dusk brought swarms of mosquitoes, and as the two of us were wearing shorts only, we were grateful for the protective covering of caked mud. On the far bank the fire danced as Charles, Peter and Anthony relaxed, doubtless with cups of steaming coffee, beneath their mosquito nets. With sudden energy, Nick dashed off down the bridge and returned after half an hour— just as I was beginning to think he had succumbed to the temptation of the camp fire—in a large rowing boat. He held a storm lantern whilst two grinning fishermen handled the oars, oblivious to the swarms of insects. Using their rope and our combined strength, we lowered the trailer over the fence until it hung suspended over the bows. It was quite definitely bigger than the boat, but no one seemed to object—not in English anyway. More by luck than good management, the stalwart fishermen evaded death by compression between their boat and the trailer, and squeezing from beneath its bulk, they retrieved their oars and poled the delicately balanced load to the far bank.

Their journey appeared fairly sedate, for the lamp glowed

steadily on the bows as we watched. They failed to return for the second trailer, and a search of the other bank revealed the trailer unloaded on firm ground, with the boat chained to a post in the reeds nearby. Our friends had had enough, tactfully doused their light, and disappeared.

We returned yet again over the four hundred yards of planking, and pushed the heavier trailer up to the bridge. With no boat and only fifty per cent better off than when we had arrived three hours earlier, we lay despondently by the fence and meditated.

Awakened from a profound reverie by the violent shaking of my shoulder, I found a little fat man, whose grubby turban was larger than his head, had arrived with a Commer wagon. It was empty, which was rare, for no one in these parts should commit the social error of taking transport, whether mule or lorry, anywhere without a full load. He said he was Achmad and that though he had travelled the Kosti road for thirty years, he had never before been delayed in such a manner. Mollified by Rothmans and a Sudan guinea, he squatted by us and surveyed the obvious problem. I think we all arrived at a possible solution simultaneously.

Another truck hove to shortly, and with twenty pairs of hands —the majority knowing that their own progress depended on our speedy dispatch—the trailer was lifted high onto the canopy of Achmad's Commer. Positioned so that its protruding side and wheel overhung the lorry on the outer side only, the crossing was made in style. The outer wall of girders on the bridge was only six feet high, and the extra width of trailer now rode free above it.

Achmad accepted his pre-arranged five guineas and accompanied us to the hovercraft camp, where the others slept soundly without a guard. He could not understand how we survived on the Horlicks rations, but sampled all the packets nevertheless, whilst expressing disgust at his liberal portion of coffee. He settled down for the night with us, but had left when we rose.

Black coffee and orange dawn—both hot and steaming. We slept naked beneath carefully stitched mosquito nets, but everything still seemed clammy on waking. Charles, always silent in the early morning, as if observing the English breakfast-hour, started the six engines, checking rev counters individually, and giving exposed electrical components their daily dose of Damp-start.

A herd of some two or three hundred camels came ambling through the reeds to our clearing, and entered the water to drink and cool their long legs. Five camel-men appeared by another path, each with his shield and broadsword slung from his scrawny shoulder. These were men of the Manaasir, a small tribe from the Northern Province, and we found their naive charm and curiosity very different from the dignified ways of our Nubian friends. They declined the offer to share our coffee, but when Anthony suggested they demonstrate their skill at arms, they readily agreed and two of their number set to for fifteen minutes of fast and furious fun. Swords flashed in vicious arcs, sighing through the air to thud against shield or short blocking-stick with mock ferocity. Their footwork was so quick and sure as they circled warily and darted in and out of the close fray as at given signals, I felt sure this must be an everyday sport to them. Eventually losing interest, the participants clasped each other's elbows to signify parity of skill, and ran down to the waterside where the Hawks' engines revved as the skirts inflated in a cloud of fine dust.

Anthony had fixed his smaller tripod to Burton's roof and filmed the sudden commotion amongst the camels as both craft slid down onto the water and away between wildly pushing groups of the ungainly beasts. The camel-men gaped, standing alert as they watched the craft disappear, then laughing with released tension and delight. Here was a story which would hold the attention of their friends and families around the clan fire for many a year. Some of their camels fled from sight through the reeds but this caused no concern.

A police van arrived as Nick and I packed last items aboard the Land-Rovers and with a cheery greeting but no explanation, dropped off a khaki-clad Nubian type who was certainly not an inch under six foot six—even without his wide-brimmed bush hat, purple ostrich feather sewn into the hatband; this was our guide. After the first futile attempts, we gave up trying to communicate, though we established that he was Corporal Omar and had instructions to get us as far as Renk. He travelled with me in the leading vehicle and proved a perfect passenger, and though he puffed away at a seemingly inexhaustible supply of fat black cigars, they had a pleasant smell that somehow reminded me of schooldays and the headmaster's study.

We reached El Jebelain by midday; the name means 'two mountains' and as we jolted wearily over the nightmarish tracks, every pair of hillocks to our front promised to shelter the village. It is a flat empty land where course dourra wheat and lucerne are grown in small patches by a few Dinka farmers. All the locals carried spears, usually two hunting shafts, rather larger than the Masai assegai, and a short hand-spear not unlike the East African panga. The road was heavily corrugated with deep recurring ruts and, wherever a crude drainage-channel passed beneath it, sharp switchback bumps had to be crossed—a painfully slow and oft-repeated process of unhitching the trailers and pulling them over manually, otherwise the tow-bars attached to the Land-Rovers became embedded in the hummocks and were the very devil to detach. The dust, too, was a problem, though fortunately there was no wind other than the draught caused in our passing, for it was red and choking and found a way round or through our shemagh headcloths and driving goggles, into the carburettors, and boxes of camera kit.

Five hours through a wilderness of tall parched grass to the little world of Paloich where various family clans of the Dinka tribe live in peaceful isolation from the rest of the world. Few of these simple retired warriors had heard of Wadi Halfa, let alone Ethiopia or Uganda—their nearest neighbours. Omar led us to a 'restoorant'!—no different in appearance to any of the other mud huts—where a long cool draught of araqi date beer, paid for in cigarettes, trickled like nectar down our dust dry throats. All the village huts were built as from a single mould; the tea-house distinguished only by a coarse reed matting inside and out, and the huge clay gourds of cool araqi or greenish water that stood beneath the thatched roof overhang in permanent shade. The menu consisted of beans and baked dourra flour. The flour balls were nourishing and our teeth crunched on numerous raisin-like particles, which, as Omar pointed out with his long and aristocratic fingers, were large weevils.

The road improved for a while after Paloich and, as dusk spread pale green opalescence over the land, warning the smaller birds and beasts that the hour of the predator approached, we passed into a region of semi-forest where baboons shuffled across the road and parrots trilled brokenly from nowhere. The road between the trees gave way to soft tracks in the sand and I was glad, as the vehicles' lights revealed a network of diverging tracks, that Omar was with us to confirm the Renk 'road'.

Through Geigar, where mangy curs snarled and snapped at the tyres, and tribesmen, their spears glinting in our lights, lined the doors of the kraals as they doubtless did whenever a vehicle passed in these parts. Here everything was an event, now that inter-tribal feuds had been stopped and the main source of activity and gossip along with them.

Our scheduled evening radio call had had no response and the sight of our three river-borne companions, when at midnight we arrived at last in Renk, was relieving. A hovercraft breakdown in some remote stretch of the river north of Renk would have really put paid to our schedule, but there was little that could go wrong which Charles could not repair in situ—amongst his many-sided achievements in his Oxcam days had been the design of his own prototype engine. He was seldom at a loss in theory or practice and proved a master at improvisation.

On reaching Renk, and finding a suitable beaching area, Charles had contacted the town's chief inspector, who had been awaiting our advent for weeks. He had arranged a sleeping place for us all and the evening meal was apparently on the house at the only restaurant in the village. This knowledge made us want to order with abandon and it was disappointing to find the choice of menu limited to Nile perch with or without beans. Tepid Coca Cola in dusty bottles with rusty tops or carafes of filtered Nile water cost the same and neither proved sufficient to wash away the acrid taste of high perch.

Peter showed us our quarters for the night, simply the compound within the walls of the police-station where we provided a fine spectacle to a huddle of emaciated prisoners. The Renk police proved more efficient or officious than their brethren farther north, for the Land-Rovers were thoroughly searched for the first time, the firearms and ammunition being removed and locked up in an empty cell.

All night long the cell inmates spat and chatted; sleep seemed unattainable in the dank throbbing heat with the malevolent whine of mosquitoes searching for some small rent in the netting or a bare limb laid carelessly close to its gauze. Even the hardened Dinka herdsmen of these parts keep cow dung fires smouldering throughout the night hours and rub the powdered ash over their bodies for protection from malaria.

Over the 19th and 20th we pressed on to Malakal, stopping a night at a remote little village called Malut; the hovercraft were making fine headway. Birds of every size and hue were in abundance from the smallest of humming-birds to the four-foot pelicans which stood on one leg and watched the intruding craft with their noisy engines as though they were a daily occurrence. Crocodile were not in evidence, possibly owing to the lack of sandy banks or other potential basking areas. Large animals of a similar appearance to otters played on muddy platforms protruding through the hyacinth. Plump herons, beaks resting on grey plumage, surveyed our passing without alarm. Too idle to fly, they travelled downstream on their private lilos, small islands of weed drifting with the current.

At midday on the 20th, some three hours after leaving Malut, Peter in the leading craft noticed an ominously dark cloud-front approaching from the south. Within an hour the floating islands of hyacinth had thickened into unbroken lines. The river was running noticeably faster, even viewed from the cockpits of the fast skimming Hawks, and forked lightning lit the sky. The storm broke with alarming speed and intensity and lasted some ten minutes before passing as quickly as it had come, leaving the river like a seething cauldron of spinach soup. Eddies of an unpredictable nature swirled knots of hyacinth violently sideways. Moisture rose like morning mist and the sun's heat redoubled after its brief absence. The cockpits' interiors resembled miniature sauna baths. We carried our filtered water in Omani 'zamzamias', porous cloth bags, in which more than three pints can be kept cool on the hottest of days. Charles, heavily built, had emptied his container long before midday and was losing sweat in streams. The controls are simple but, with haphazard logs and vegetation flotsam swirling from the storm, both the driver's hands were kept busy between steering corrections and the three throttle levers, which required delicate alterations from time to time to counter the ever-changing surface and wind conditions. A hand used to wipe sweat away from the driver's eyes at the wrong moment could induce a weaving movement in the Hawk's course—not a good idea when moving at some twenty knots between the bank and islands of floating brushwood.

Wide open fields with lightly spattered Dinka kraals here and there—for the most part deserted. After endless miles in the ulu, the Malakal airstrip came as a surprise with its modern concrete structure, radio antennae and wire fences, brightly coloured Shell/B.P. tanker lorries parked on the hot white apron. The town stretches away to the south and hugs the river with avenues of shady palms. To approach by river is a sight never to forget, for here is the Nile of the explorer's day, known and loved by Governor Baker and Gordon Pasha.

Dwarfing the little Hawks, ancient paddle-steamers were moored to the overgrown banks, their cracked lattice shutters slowly swinging and creaking with the movement of a faint swell. They had weathered successive floods, long since disused though they were, and green lichen on their timber blended with the deep purple rust of the metal work. From their gaping windows and the low rotting passenger-decks, there plunged and screamed shiny naked bodies of the natives, young and old, all happy in their poor man's funfair. Their cloaks, nearly always of a fine red dye, and their prized personal spears, lay discarded over the boat's woodwork, a mutual trust precluding theft much as it does amongst European skiers when they leave their expensive skis propped outside Alpine 'hot chocolate, gluhwein, and goodies' restaurants. Here bundles of hippopotamus hide in long thin slices were being rolled to crude storage shelters by chanting Shilluks, their faces and shoulders thick with tribal cicatrices. Arabs in clean white robes, always clean, supervised from grubby notebooks with gold sheathed pens as dourra grain was weighed and sifted. Only the slaves, the glistening heaps of ivory, and the khaki-clad district commissioner were missing; otherwise the scene was complete, as I had always imagined it should be.

No district commissioner; no white men at all; indeed, between Khartoum and Uganda we never saw a European other than a family of Greek shopkeepers in Malakal who had been there for thirty years and spoke the Shilluk tongue as well as their half-naked creditors.

Malakal is the capital of the Upper Nile Province and of all the Shilluk territories. Here we spent two days and with the aid of the local director of education, Dr. Mortaseen, arranged to film the little-known Bar-Deng witch-doctor rituals and the tribal drum dances of the Shilluk. Unfortunately the Security Police got wise to our intentions and vetoed our filming activities—Dr. Mortaseen receiving an imperial dressing-down and warning from the pompous inspector who had taken over watchdog duties from Omar. We protested violently and waved our permit at him, pointing out that whatever he might think was forbidden, Khartoum had already and only recently given us photographic carte blanche in the South. His reply was to show us an instruction received from the Ministry of the Interior that very morning, forbidding any form of photography in all the southern provinces by anyone without special government permission. This, I told him, was precisely what we had. He laughed and repeated his orders that our cameras were to be left alone until we had left the country and that any transgressions of this edict would result in our arrest as spies.

All provincial capital towns in the South have a local Security Committee which acts as a petty government and without the authority of which virtually nothing can be done. The committee consists of the Government Inspector, who is really a District Commissioner under a less tainted title, together with the local Police and Army Commanders. This system keeps a fairly close check on the activities of the military though, in the light of the September 1969 military coup, not close enough. It also means the conflicting personalities of the three wise men—who would

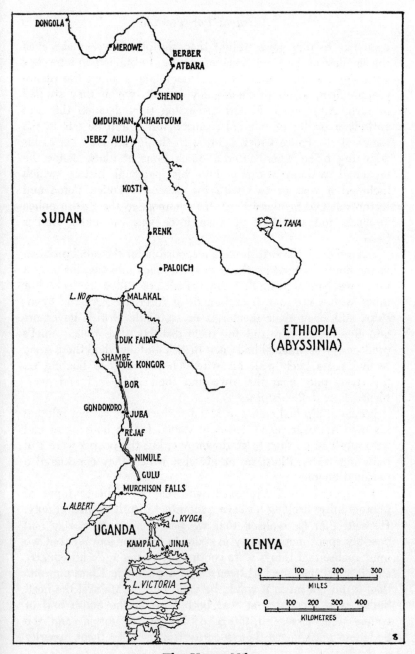

The Upper Nile

each like to pull more weight than the other two—make even
the smallest of decisions time-consuming. I obtained an interview
with the Malakal Committee and complained about the photographic ban, again producing my permit, which they studied
in turn. After much heated discussion they decided this was
entirely a matter of internal security and would be left in the
hands of the Police Chief. I left with the latter and went to his
adjoining office where after a quick bout of black coffee, he
launched without warning into his personal history which
included a year or two with the Leicester Police Force and
lectures at Old Scotland Yard. He commended the British police
methods and said that his own force was run along similar
lines.

Even though the British were responsible for the rebel problem
in the South; he told us, there was still much affection for us as a
race—we had noticed that the British are called 'ingleezi' but
other whites are known as faranji, or foreigners. All the townships still have their memories of erstwhile British governors
and the things they did for their districts. The police chief's
predecessor in Malakal had been British and had died there some
twelve years back with his wife. They had gone boating on
the river quite near the town and their little skiff had over-
turned in a sudden storm.

Prince Philip had called in Malakal three days earlier, piloting
his own Andover plane. He only stayed for an hour or so and
naturally had no time to go downtown, but the people were still
bubbling with enthusiasm at his visit which they considered a
personal honour.

The police chief discussed with us the delicate topic of
photography, stroking his severe moustache with studied gravity.
He said that he realised that we had come a long way and
possibly spent much money in order to film our journey, but we
must realise that things were continually changing in his country
and just because we had been given a permit in Khartoum one
day, it did not mean it would be valid here in Malakal the next.
Sudan was a country at war both here in the South and of
course with Israel, so things could not be normal and the
Sudanese must guard their security jealously. To them, security

Shilluk children by the River Sobat.


The ferry at Juba.

Burton is transferred to a more elevated position after a trailer's suspension broke.

The area north of Nimule has been totally depopulated, or so it appeared.

did not only concern military secrets, for, should we film the natives without any clothes and then slant our film commentary from a critical angle, this could do the Government much harm. We might try to use such photographs as evidence that the Southerners were being oppressed and impoverished. However, he felt that we were to be trusted, for we would hardly have arrived in so sensational a manner if our intentions had been subversive. He ended by saying that we might take photographs and films of the machines as long as they remained on or near the Nile and the background contained no naked people nor military installations. We would leave it at that, and would so inform his colleagues farther south. He then poured us out some thick black coffee which was delicious.

He promised to send a well-armed escort with our road party and one of his police captains to ensure our well-being. We must not under-estimate the dangers of the route for his patrol convoys still suffered the occasional ambush in the Bor forest area and of course the country south of Juba, which is heavily wooded and ideal guerilla country. Bridges and tracks had often been mined and lone rebel machine-gunners still inflicted damage from the undergrowth by the main tracks, although the army were on the face of it—in control of the area and the larger rebel groups kept to the swamp country and the remote forests.

I left the government buildings and wandered down to the river, reflecting that the police chief had at least given us the thin end of the wedge. Photography by the riverside is enough when all life and customs are drawn to the river, as in the Sudan. And of course there was no telling how permissive our new police watchdog would become once we had left Malakal and shared our whisky generously enough to soothe his conscience. Things could really have been much worse, I felt.

Charles and Peter had arranged a demonstration on a muddy slope between the lines of moored paddle-steamers. The place was quite clear of hyacinth blockage whenever the wind blew from the east and from this launching point they had already explored upstream for a considerable distance towards Lake No at which point the river becomes the Bahr el Jebel and the true swamps begin.

L

The word had spread of our arrival and by the time the government inspector, police chief and other local dignitaries arrived, a frighteningly large crowd of town natives and tribesmen from the surrounding area had congregated on the bank. The noise and brilliant, contrasting colours of the robes reminded me of Ascot races, except that here the topless and the micro-skirted were very much in evidence. Anthony, standing on the cabin of a Land-Rover, with his ciné camera was visible over the bobbing heads, making hay while the sun shone, for here were examples of every tribal type and dress and we were within our photographic limits after all. The gay coloured plumes of military bush hats—purple, orange and yellow—dotted the crowd, for five steamers had arrived that morning from the south with soldiers on leave from the battle-zone west of Juba.

I heard the familiar mini-roar of the Hawks' little engines and shouldered my way through the heaving throng, coming on occasions in solid contact with the bouncing bare breasts of excited female spectators, much to my embarrassment and their apparent amusement.

A sudden near-silence followed by a general utterance of what sounded very like 'Wow' or—to Sudanise this Americanism— 'Wau', and then an ecstatic cheering whilst spears and items of clothing flew into the air. I joined Anthony on the vehicle cab and only then realised the full size of the crowd. There were Dinkas, Shilluks, Nuer, even the light-skinned Azande. Some had scaled the lofty trees by the waterside, others clung to the rotting running-boards of the steamers, or pushed forward by those on the banks, stood up to their waists in the muddy shallows.

Both Hawks were now skidding merrily over the weed-strewn surface, Charles amusing himself, and by the lusty cries of some two thousand spectators, pleasing the onlookers, with a series of figures-of-eights perilously close to the steamers. Baker's skirt became snarled by a thick tangle of floating vegetation and Peter taxied over the hyacinth onto the muddy landing strip intending to disentangle the weeds. A dozen or so of the local militia were busy with their rhino-hide batons keeping the landing area free, but as Peter surged out of the water, a sigh of wonder at the magical performance of these strange craft was the sign for a general scrabble at the back of the mêlée. The resulting pressure at the front rendered the police quite inadequate and, in the ensuing confusion, I caught a glimpse of Peter's horrified expression as he swung the steering wheel wildly in a vain attempt to avoid the human wall closing in on him.

A sudden scream, cut off suddenly, an ugly shriek of pain, and then my own hoarse shouts as I fought through the bewildered spectators. As I reached the waterside, the Hawk slid back slowly into the black mud; Peter had left the lift engine going although he had immediately cut both drive motors on seeing his predicament. This meant no-one could be crushed beneath the craft since the air cushion still supported its weight. Numerous naked children had been placed at the front of the crowd by their parents, to see the fun, and by some lucky chance Peter had managed to turn the craft before ploughing into the main body of them; but as the Hawk slewed round it had literally scooped a group of the smaller children onto its running board and dragged them into the thick black mud beneath its skirt.

Frantically, with a suffocating shower of mud from the Hawk to make vision impossible, Nick and I scrabbled in the slime. A policeman pulled a little arm from below the skirt and, though dark blood ran mingling with the filth, the child was still alive. We pushed Baker carefully into deeper water where Peter could safely switch off, and the craft slowly lowered into the water without danger of crushing anybody who might still be trapped below the skirt. The police had meanwhile retrieved a second child from the shallows, vomiting and badly shocked, but seemingly uninjured. There was no means of telling how many had been dragged beneath the water, but the area, where bodies might still have been, was full of police searching and prodding the depths. Others had now cleared a space where both Hawks landed and Charles joined us to hear the unhappy news. The crowd were beginning to chant in anger and shock, as the police tried to disperse them. The situation seemed unpleasant and I was relieved when a Peugeot van arrived with its hooter blaring, a crudely scrawled red cross on its flank and blankets in the rear compartment—Malakal's ambulance. Inspector Joseph Samuel introduced himself as the ambulance drew up and suggested that we all went back to the hospital with the injured for he felt that our continued presence would hardly help what could become an ugly situation. There were three injured children, and we left with them through the grumbling throng.

There was a sort of out-patients ward where the ambulance stopped and a male nurse arrived to carry the injured inside. One of the children had lost half an ear, the others seemed to have internal injuries and various small cuts. Nothing serious, Inspector Samuel assured us, so we returned to our Land-Rovers much relieved. The crowds had gone when further searches had produced no corpses, and Inspector Samuel said there would be no danger from the tribesmen. Tempers die down as quickly us they flare, he explained, and the police had made it quite clear that we would be punished should we be found to blame for the accident.

We retired for the night, feeling that the episode was closed and hoping to be on our way to Bor early the next morning. Achmad, Omar's successor, put paid to our hopes. He arrived at ten o'clock that night and, leering his unpleasant smirk, informed Peter he was under arrest and was to report at once to the town police headquarters.

# CHAPTER 11

∞

## *Rebel Forests*

"Our law is still that of the British Administration, and we have found no clause which adequately deals with legal procedure to be taken against someone causing an accident in circumstances like those of yesterday.

"The accident was caused neither by a boat nor a road vehicle, and there appears to be no legislation against hovering vehicles, an omission of which I must inform Khartoum."

The Malakal J.P., a stocky Nubian type, had summoned Peter to his presence the preceding night, only to postpone the appointment—probably still searching feverishly for a law dealing with hovercraft—and thereby also delaying our departure. When His Lordship eventually got round to conceding defeat and explaining the premature summons to Peter, the latter apologised for the mishap but pointed out that it would not have occurred had there been sufficient police to control the crowd, since it was the crowd and not Baker that had lost control.

The judge admitted this, but pointed out that the law had to be very discreet in the South since the people realise that the great majority of barristers are from the North and so are quick to cause an outcry if any public offence against one of their number is not dealt with as severely as it would be in the North. The laws are strict with traffic offenders, and had he ignored yesterday's affair, there would have been objections from many quarters. But our arrest had been made public which should suffice to satisfy any potential objectors; though since we did not seem to have transgressed any standing law, he would not after all press charges.

Peter's reappearance unfettered was heartening, but we suffered a further disappointment when Inspector Paul Joseph arrived in the midst of our preparations to leave what Nick was already describing as the scene of the crime.

He had come, he said, at the bidding of the Security Committee. Three grain trucks had returned to Malakal the night before, having failed to make the journey through to Mogoch, a smallish village some ninety miles to the south. The rains had begun in those regions and the tracks south of Malakal were now officially closed, since any vehicle bogged in the swamplands would have to be abandoned for the next seven months. Our plans to hover to Bor were quite out of the question as all tracks leading to the river were now submerged and refuelling at such 'riverside' villages as Jonglei was therefore impossible. Bogged Land-Rovers meant no fuel for the Hoverhawks so to our chagrin we would have to carry on solely by land whilst the way was still open.

Seeing our downcast expressions, the Inspector added that the Security Committee was sympathetic to our plight and since the Khartoum authorities had asked for every help to be given to ease our journey, they had withheld an army convoy due to leave that morning for an outpost near Bor.

The convoy was to be commanded by a young lieutenant, and would consist of two large Mercedes trucks with some twenty heavily-armed soldiers; it would be the last detachment to leave Malakal for the south that year, and the lieutenant had orders to return if the going became too bad. What we did would be up to us, but we should remember that the whole area would soon be a vast lake larger than England, and no Automobile Association could extricate us, once bogged, even if there was one.

The river between Bor and Fenikang is up to twenty-one miles wide in places, even in the dry season. It is a meandering network of dank waterways, one of the world's most inhospitable regions. Only the best river-pilots who have traversed the area many times can afford to be confident in the swamps, for the watercourse is forever changing, and a single storm can alter the geography of the terrain overnight by breaking off whole islands of stinking vegetation and piling uprooted banks of reed and ambatch one upon the other, crushing and suffocating anything in the way. Dead crocodiles and hippo float bloated in the newly formed streams after such storms, and elephants wander starving on islands which were earlier part of the swampy mainland.

Steamers can complete the journey to Juba in under a week when the channel has recently been cleared, but less than a century ago it was considered something of a miracle when Samuel Baker sailed from Khartoum to Gondokoro near Juba in only a month. Other less determined expeditions never reappeared after entering the 'sudd'—an apt name which comes from the Arabic verb meaning to block.

There was no alternative but to count our losses, join the convoy, and hope to reach Bor and the southern rim of the swamp-lands before being cut off by the impending floods, which would mean leaving all the equipment and, as Peter sardonically commented, a long swim. In retrospect, it was as well we left when we did. As it was, we reached Bor only two days before the rains set in over the swamps, and only then by abandoning much of the equipment en route.

The lieutenant sent an impatient note to say he was waiting at the southern end of town, so we hurriedly hitched the Hawks back on to their trailers, the springs of which sank alarmingly, and bounced off southwards, crossing the River Sobat east of Fenikang on a ferry which was only wide enough for our trailers after an angry skipper had agreed, under military pressure, to remove part of the superstructure of his wheel-house.

South of the Sobat was a desolate bush country; our track winding through strangely silent woods, many miles without a sign of life, though well-used trails led off into the scrub as though we had only to wait to see the occupants of this mysterious region. I felt certain our passage was being observed, although if there were hidden watchers, they gave no hint of their presence.

The woods yielded to wide clearings from time to time where crops had once grown. A Stonehenge in miniature, partly overgrown by thorn bush, decorated one such clearing. Achmad told us this was a Dinka rain shrine, though he had earlier said these swamp-lands were Nuer country of the Lau and Twae tribes. He explained that most of the southern tribes have rain-makers; a sort of tribal insurance against drought. Although the rain-maker is a man of some standing in any village, his is not an enviable task. The Nuer tribes are kind to their rain-makers, but the Dinka and Shilluk kill theirs from time to time to appease the Gods. They consider rain-makers to be divine beings inhabited by tribal spirits, and after a time of drought, or whenever a change in rain-makers is desirable, they bury them alive or strangle them slowly with reed ropes. The Madi roast theirs over a slow fire and collect the fat from the body to heal their wounds. The Bari people, on the other hand, believe that many of their number have inherent rain-making talents, and so appoint quite a few in each village. If they do well, they are allowed to die normally, and their corpses are carefully plugged before burial, reeds being placed in all the body orifices to prevent their spirits escaping. But a bad Bari rain-maker will be stabbed, and his belly ripped open for the birds to finish off. Apart from hereditary rigmaroles involving animal sacrifice, the rain-makers have special sets of quartz stones which they rub with various potions to influence the rain-clouds.

Achmad's tones were suitably derisive, whenever lecturing us on the customs of the Southerners, to indicate his own disbelief in their backward practices.

Dusk settled and Achmad argued with the lieutenant who wanted to push on during the night. The sky was ominously dark to the south, true enough, and the soil was malleable porous clay which indicated, by the deeply-etched tyre ruts, how treacherous it was likely to become when wet.

I felt the first drops of rain on my elbow soon before nightfall and the steady drizzle which set in was not long in becoming a drumming downpour which made conversation difficult. The road resembled wet putty and whenever the smaller trailer's wheels skidded into the deep ruts, its axle became embedded as the wheels just didn't reach the bottom of the ruts; the other trailer, having bigger wheels, caused no trouble. As the putty became sludge, the wheels sunk deeper and the smaller trailer complained bitterly with a shrill note of metallic friction, whilst shaking itself, the Land-Rover and the Hawk with shuddering vibrations by running its undercarriage along the centre of the track. There was a puncture in a trailer tyre, and the sudden jolt as its load sunk lopsided, wrenching the tow-bar and cracking its hook-link like so much papier mâché. The Land-Rover's rear half-shaft snapped simultaneously and inexplicably.

Any vehicle without four-wheel drive would have had difficulty pulling itself through that mire even without a heavy-laden trailer; so we had no choice but to abandon the trailer with its broken tow-bar, and heave Baker onto the leading Mercedes lorry. The lieutenant had other ideas.

"It will take far too long and every minute counts now—if we are to get through. Anyway you will never lift that thing high enough to get it on." As the rain poured down and the soldiers, huddled miserably over dripping submachine-guns, glared at us as though we were the sole reason for their discomfort, Charles hovered the Hawk off its stricken trailer, over the slimy track, and between the two lorries, where he cut the engines and Baker sunk—like Quatermass into the Pit. This seemed to decide the soldiers, now that they had seen something of the wonders of the Hawk, they knew that such a machine could hardly be left abandoned. Without reference to their lieutenant, they clambered down from the trucks, and with a dozen on each side of Baker, chanting in the downpour, we managed to heave the heavy craft—from which rivulets of liquid mud streamed—high onto the soldiers' equipment bundles in the back of the Mercedes. Charles offered to travel with Baker to keep an eye on the Hawks, but the lieutenant would not countenance any of us travelling in Sudan Army vehicles.

At intervals along the track we came upon three deserted lorries. To get round each was a major task, as by now the sodden clay was thicker than any I had seen, like that of a Sussex bog but more glutinous for it clung limpet-like to our boots when pushing, and great blats of the muck on our soles had us walking like astronauts on the moon. Progress was only possible in first gear and four-wheel drive; in silent frustration we advanced through the nightmarish quagmire until, towards four in the morning, the lieutenant called a halt by a patch of high ground that turned out to be Mogoch. Achmad awoke from his slumber and billeted himself in the largest of the little huts of the village; he was still partially dry since he had neither pushed nor helped in any way. The villagers of Mogoch, all five of them, looked a sorry lot, and told us that nothing had come through from the south for two weeks, so they had no idea whether the track got better or worse.

The lieutenant, who had made the overland journey to Bor once before in the dry season—he usually travelled by troop steamer—told us that a ridge of higher ground known as the Duk ran parallel to the river and some forty miles east of the main channel. Once the track reached it, he felt we should make better progress and with luck arrive at Bor by nightfall. The Bor tribe, like the Twae—meaning Thunderbolt—and many smaller tribes in the marshes, are all of the Dinka family and their domain stretches from Renk in the north to well south of Juba. The river Dinka tribes are mainly cattlemen, but their poorer relatives, the Than tribesmen, live on elevated patches deep in the marshes, where hippo and fish allow them a threadbare existence.

We left Magoch soon after dawn at the instigation of the lieutenant, who was as anxious as ever to push on. The mosquitoes had kept us from sleeping, in spite of fatigue, but I had trouble waking Achmad who lay full-length, with his spectacles on and his beloved submachine-gun cradled between his knees, on a comfortable-looking, though moth-eaten, car seat in his self appointed billet. The deluge had abated, though the sky remained overcast, and we made faster progress that morning though the second trailer had to be left by the way-side (its suspension having finally and irreparably given up the ghost) and Burton heaved onto the second Mercedes. By midday we had reached the higher ground of the Duk; not so much a visible rise as the result of a gradual climb over the last few miles which sufficed to take the track above the level of the watershed. The deep ruts were still in evidence, but now their floor was more or less firm and we could motor in second gear without low ratio, which doubled our rate of progress. The very firmness of the ground caused a new obstacle; a series of deep puddles in the track, some two or three feet deep and sometimes as long as Brighton Pier is wide. The old diesel vehicle with its broken half-shaft floundered hopelessly in the deeper of these pools and, since we couldn't, Achmad excepted, get any dirtier, we waded out and pushed.

We passed Duk Kongor, Duk Fadiat, and other smaller villages clusters of beehive huts with large domed thatch roofs rising to steeply finished points. The larger and more luxurious ones housed the cattle, according to Achmad. Unlike others we had noticed in the scrubland around Mogoch, these had normal sunken foundations, whereas those on lower land were built on gnarled stilts which kept their dung floors well above the level of the annual floods.

The folk of Duk Fadiat were congregated beneath a shady sycamore in the centre of the hamlet and surveyed our passing with interest. All were naked apart from a wealth of multi-coloured beads around their midriffs, and presented the strangest of sights. A large number of both sexes were well over six foot four, and beautifully proportioned. An old gaffer with a home-made pipe and tattered sailor's hat approached us with an expression of joy, almost of recognition, and doffing his cap repeatedly, wished us a "Very good morning sahs", in the quaintest of Jeevesian accents. So dignified was his manner, it was easy to forget that he was stark naked except for his Popeye head-dress. The place lent itself to a short pause for photography, and a lengthy argument with Achmad and the lieutenant ensued since both of them considered nudity obscene and definitely not something to be photographed.

Gnashing our teeth in frustration, we continued our race with the rains, and soon left the Duk behind us, though fortunately the track had now been built up by some long-past and industrious administration so that the marshes lay at a lower level to either side of us. In places the built-up soil had partially subsided back into the bog, so that it was hardly wide enough for the trucks to pass. Two small bulldozing vehicles were operating not far south of the Duk but they had only partially succeeded in flattening the ruts. A convoy of some fifteen army lorries, which Achmad said would be the last to try the journey north that year, roared past us and reduced the track to its former pitted state, as though the bulldozers had never been there. Wearily we pushed and towed to get the vehicles out of the ditch into which we had been forced by the convoy.

Black storm clouds of a vicious density ranged over the bleak marshlands to the south and east; dark patches wherein lightning flickered, and a background of continuous thunder made us thankful we had heeded the lieutenant's advice to press on. Dreading the first heavy drops of rain, which would turn the track to a waterlogged runnel in an hour of deluge, we drove as fast as was safely possible, keeping an eye on the ominous thunder-clouds to our front.

Achmad became excited as a long dark crestline edged the southern horizon. "Bor Forest!" he exclaimed. The forest is only nine miles from the town, and although it is laced with gulleys for the flood waters, the bridges are kept in good condition by the tribes living in the forest who need flour and other goods from Bor, and so replace the bridging planks each time they are swept away by the floods.

The forest itself used to be the centre of the Anya Nya's rebellious activities and many a convoy has been ambushed there. Small groups are still a danger but they are usually careful not to harm the rare foreigner that comes this way for fear of damaging their cause abroad. They are supported by many countries and unofficially by their neighbours, the Ugandans, as well as world-wide Roman Catholic movements.

"If we make the southern edge of the forest where the ground is higher before the storms break," said Achmad, "we will have no further worries."

The escort lorries had long since dropped out of sight behind us. We felt the obvious need to remain at least in sight of the Army lorries with their precious burdens, but the track would soon become impassable if we delayed and the storm cut us off from Bor. Better to risk the Hoverhawks than hang around for the lorries and so risk losing the Land-Rovers and equipment as well. Also, although slower, the lorries had much larger tyres and better traction on swampy ground. Achmad was clearly for pressing on to the comforts of Bor Police Headquarters, and was anyway of the opinion that the lorries offered a more attractive

target for a rebel ambush than ourselves. Nevertheless he cocked
his sten-gun, and Nick followed his example, making the 7.62
F.N. ready, with six full magazines to hand.

We reached the outskirts of the forest, a dank, gloomy place
with thick foliage enclosing the track and grotesquely mildewed
branches entwining overhead—which reminded me of the Hawks
travelling high on the trucks. I dreaded to think how the glass-
fibre cockpits would react to the battering they would doubtless
receive from these overhanging boughs. We were deep into the
forest when the storm broke over us, and though the foliage took
the main force of the deluge, the noise was deafening. Blackened
tree trunks in the forest were mute witnesses to the damage
inflicted by past storms, but no lightning struck near us; the
windscreen wipers were inadequate as the vehicles skidded over
the slippery mud, only the ruts keeping us from slewing into the
mire which formed the forest floor to either side. Each deepening
pool through which we thudded sent cascades of slime onto the
windscreens. I noticed with secret pleasure a muddy trickle
from the front wind vent blowing a thin red stream onto
Achmad's seat. It would soon make him as wet as the rest of
us, but he didn't seem to comprehend the workings of the
simple vent lever which would have put a stop to his tribulations.

We crossed a series of wooden bridges, some with loose and
rotten logging and shortly before dusk an ecstatic sigh from the
weary Achmad signalled our arrival at Bor, startling in its
sudden rural appearance after the wild scenes of the forest.

Achmad took us straight to the police headquarters, an
unpretentious private house near the river-bank. After lengthy
salaams to all and sundry and doubtless long descriptions of his
hazardous journey from Malakal with the English spies, he
returned with a police friend to find us all asleep in the vehicles.
They took us to a hut with fly wiring—one of the few, Achmad
pointed out, which had not had its roof removed by a recent
storm—and we wearily spread damp sleeping bags and Horlicks
packs on the concrete floor. No great comfort was needed to
induce sleep, and for the first time we dispersed with mosquito
nets and camp beds through an overwhelming desire for
immediate oblivion. The local police chief called at an

unpleasantly early hour the next day, the 24th, with the news that one Mercedes had arrived at three in the morning and offloaded its Hawk by the riverside. Of the other there was still no sign.

We hurried down to the river and found Burton squatting forlornly amidst a crowd of young admirers and soon saw that the rear fibreglass rim was extensively cracked, and the hover-skirt attachment liners split in many places; the cabin too was battered on either side and a sorry sight, overhanging branches and careless handling were no doubt the cause. Charles began his repairs at once, cursing the carelessness of Sudanese soldiers in general, and our escort in particular though this was hardly fair since without their help we would never have left Malakal. The second lorry was towed into Bor later that day. Black mud clung to its sides and, to our dismay, also to Baker's right flank. It transpired that a bridge had collapsed under the lorry, and an army winch-truck from the Bor 'barracks' had been called out with thirty extra soldiers, before it could be hauled out of the stream with its undercarriage damaged. During the course of the recovery, Baker had been removed from the truck, doubtless with speed and neglect, and the consequent damage was con-siderable. The lift engine assembly and complete fan unit had been ripped from their housing with the chassis and left hanging by an intricate maze of wiring. The rear rim of the craft was damaged beyond repair and the metal framework split laterally.

Repairs were unthinkable and further transport impossible. This was a bitter blow, especially considering our proximity to Uganda and the river's source. We detached all units of any value from Baker; a sad task since we had grown attached to the machine. Baker's empty hulk will no doubt lie on the bank there for many a year yet, amidst a scrap yard of old dugout canoes, the old and the new, soon both to become part of the history of man's ingenuity. Canoes, hovercraft, sputniks, and mooncraft — all milestones in our progress. Heaven knows what the Bor tribesmen will be gaping at in the two-thousand-seventies.

Bor, like Malakal, gives no glimpse of the great marshland that lies between them. True the hyacinth is evident, and giant papyrus and ambatch luxuriate along the banks when the natives allow them to; but the river is kept within its banks even at flood times, and the village has the feeling of an island bounded by swamps and to the south vast forests of game, domain of the little known Bari and Lotuko-speaking tribes. Bor means ditch or flooded in the Dinka tongue, since all the surrounding lands are liable to flood, but around the town itself shady avenues of sycamore lend a theme of order to the squat bungalows of the semi-rich. Across a well-shaded playground, where the townsfolk wander and gossip, the district commissioner and police chief have their headquarters in the offices of their British predecessors.

Having dispensed with the army escort, Achmad now felt solely responsible for us and our welfare, and we made it clear to him that our greatest need was to acquire a boat large enough to fit us and our equipment on board and to be on our way to Juba as soon as possible; not through any aversion to Bor and its people, but Peter and Nick were already overdue at their jobs. Unless some means were found of reaching Juba within the week, they could hardly hope to reach Nairobi by the 30th; the date when a Hercules transport plane was leaving on which they could obtain a free and speedy passage back to Britain. Charles, Anthony and I intended to continue as best we could to Jinja, the source of the Nile, where the Hawks were to provide a demonstration on Lake Victoria in early April.

Through Achmad and the army major, we sent telegrams north and south beseeching the authorities to send us some form of ferry or steamer. We never discovered what became of these telegrams, but received as much acknowledgment as if they had never been sent, and the commissioner thought it quite likely that his town's only radio transmitter had been damaged in the recent storms. He didn't appear to mind much if it had been.

With no means of driving south, since the commissioner had cheerfully told us the roads had remained closed, with all the bridges blown by rebels or washed away by floods, since early 1965, we were hamstrung and even local touring had been vetoed by the security-conscious Achmad.

Much of our time was spent in the palatial, though virtually unfurnished, residence of the commissioner. He was a kindly but indolent man who spent most of his days sipping coffee in his office whilst listening sympathetically to the innumerable petty petitions of his villagers. Over his head a punkah (fan) swished dully on its British-inspired rigging; and outside, tugging a frayed rope, squatted a dirty youth with a Yukon haircut. The imperialists have gone, but not their ways.

The commissioner was a well-educated and much travelled man. Bor, was for him the last of a long succession of outposts and he resignedly accepted its limitations, making the best of circumstances.

Our arrival was a godsend to him; with Peter he played long games of backgammon; with Charles and Nick he discussed world politics and his own local problems; with Anthony he arranged ready repairs for his long-useless ciné camera and light meter. For my part, I listened fascinated to his tales of strange customs and ritual savagery in those regions to which he had earlier been posted; the lands of the Topotha, not far from the Abyssinian border.

He told us that many of the settlements which had caused him the most trouble contained men of Galla extraction, a race of low intelligence found mostly in south-western Ethiopia. Amongst their less pleasant customs, they castrate victims of feudal or tribal murder and tie their trophies to a special waist-belt thereby theoretically gaining in their own sexual prowess. Old women suspected of sorcery have their kidneys torn out; carriers of contagious diseases are herded with their families into burning kraals, spears discouraging escape. Blunt stakes are used to stave in the chests of enemy fallen in battle and found to be wounded.

Even the children have vicious games; the Abyssinian youth who can hold a burning coal the longest gains the esteem of his fellows.

From our expedition stores the commissioner 'borrowed' vehicle spares for his aged Land-Rover, and water filters which he said he would evaluate and if he found them suitable, suggest to the Minister of Hygiene that a bulk order be made. In return, our

Young Ugandans gaze in perplexity at Burton.

Burton speeds over the mirror-smooth surface of Lake Victoria.

Jinja — source of the longest river in the world.

The hydro-electric dam at Jinja where once the Owen Falls roared over cliffs to announce the birth of the Nile.

provender improved considerably, being supplemented by mangoes, pawpaws, and breadfruit from his garden—five acres of rambling cultivation tended by a dozen naked Nuer gardeners. Mahogany, neem, ebony, and mango trees provided shade for young orange and lime sprigs. Ten days earlier the pride of the commissioner's tree collection, a giant sycamore, had been blown down in a violent storm along with some hundreds of corrugated tin sheets from the roofs of his recently erected community buildings.

When not helping Charles with the remaining Hawk or accepting the commissioner's hospitality, we wandered round the village and its environs with Achmad. He was still immensely security conscious; anyone naked was obscene, any modern building 'military' and so not much was left to photograph. However, he gave way eventually to our continued heckling and allowed a certain amount of carefully censored film to be taken of the local industries, the making of reed ropes and the shaping of ebony walking-sticks with rhino-tooth tips. The village cattle market was alive with flies and thickly carpeted with years of dung. I wondered why the commissioner hadn't made use of it for his garden. Several of the penned cows, their curving horns over two feet in length, had large pieces of flesh torn from their flanks, which Achmad put down to wolves and hyenas. Anthrax, he said, was another menace in the area, which affects the Dinkas as well as their cattle, for even though a rich tribesman may own two thousand head, he will seldom kill the beasts for meat, preferring to eat his beef only when one of the cows dies. Since they die fairly frequently of anthrax, this unpleasant disease is the cause of many agonising deaths amongst the Dinka.

The death of one of their cows is a matter of mourning and a feeling of personal loss to the Dinka cattle-owners, more than in the other tribes, for their whole way of life is centred round their favourite cows. When they die, their owners will sit in silence and refuse to eat the meat. Yet only a few hundred miles to the south of the Dinka lands, their cousins the Masai, happily slice chunks of raw meat from living oxen, avoiding only the vital arteries of the poor beasts, and their appetites are no doubt

177

improved by the bellowing of their victim as it dies in slow agony.

The Dinkas we saw were a handsome people, usually recogniseable by their exceptionally fine build. Their lower incisors are knocked out when they reach puberty, at which time they also receive their tribal scarring. Until married, the young men often wear gaily coloured beads wound tightly round their waists and necks. Ostrich and eagle feathers protrude from their red dyed mops—their Sunday-best for visiting town—which contrasts strangely with the grey of their faces which they rub carefully with dung-fire ashes as a mosquito protective.

Feuds between the Dinka and the neighbouring Moralay tribes were frequent, though they had been quelled for a while in the 1950s, and many were the fearsome tales Achmad told us of month-long police patrols in the swamp-lands to bring to book parties of tribal raiders. The Moralay were the worst he said; much bedevilled by syphilis and other endemic diseases, they lived off their raiding parties, carrying off women, children and cattle when they got the chance, sometimes in areas hundreds of miles from their own homes. Similar to the Masai of Kenya, they live mainly on a diet of beans, milk and blood from living cattle.

Achmad believed the Shilluk to be very much the most civilised of the southern tribes, and had had little trouble when working in the Shilluk lands south of the river Sobat.

The Shilluk, he said, had their own paramount chief who is known as the 'ret', and is to all intents and purposes the king of all the Shilluk sub-tribes although they in turn are ruled by local chiefs. Their craftsmanship is finer than any found in other parts of the South, certain tribes excelling at wood carvings, others at ironwork and stone grinding. Roof thatching of expertise and great durability is the hallmark of the Shilluk dwellings, and their fishing rafts of reed and ambatch will carry heavy loads, but can when empty be carried on the shoulder of a single man.

One of their more curious customs, which Achmad thought had died out now that such things are frowned upon, was the treatment of the 'ret' by his wives when old age rendered him impotent or badly ill: they would throttle him whilst he slept or else shut him up with one of their number in a cattle byre to die of thirst or suffocation. A very sensible custom really, since it made way for a younger and more effective ruler, and who to judge better when a man has reached his nadir than his own wives? In matters of love and marriage too, the Shilluk show wisdom above that of other Southerners. Young girls choose their own husbands and reach their final decision only after testing and eliminating numerous potential grooms. They may have a dozen affairs before they will be thought to be unduly flirtatious. Young love is rife in the kraals of the Shilluk and is usually ignored by sensible parents. However should the in-laws prove troublesome, there is always the local witch-doctor, usually a eunuch; it was the Shilluk medicine men who originated the practice of sticking pins into effigies of people that get in the way.

At five a.m. on the 27th, having resigned ourselves to the prospect of a prolonged stay in Bor, and Nick to being sacked by his London employers, we were woken by the long-drawn-out moan of a Thames-side foghorn from the direction of the old steamer moorings. Just then no Stradivarius violin could have produced a finer note.

# CHAPTER 12

∞

## *Jinja Moon*

Donning shorts and sandals, Nick and I ran to the quay to find a small tugboat with a full cargo of sacks of dourra flour waiting for the labour gangs' arrival for unloading to begin; once the news of its presence spread to the outlying villages, the town would soon be invaded by the tribesmen and their families, all desperate to claim their rations from the Indian store-keepers before supplies ran out for, once the rains came, the little dourra steamers would visit only on rare and unpredictable occasions.

The tug pulled two flat barges, one on either side, and a cursory glance assured us that, if perched carefully on the deck hatches of either barge, the Land-Rovers could be lashed in comparative safety and taken to Juba. The skipper, a pleasant-looking Nubian, objected flatly to the idea, and ignored our entreaties.

Further argument with the stubborn skipper was obviously a waste of time and, since he was intending to leave Bor for Juba as soon as the dourra had been unloaded, time was crucial. We visited the commissioner and interrupted his morning tea to have him intervene with the skipper. After much heated discussion and resigned gestures, the latter eventually agreed to take us south, but warned us that his boat was both slow and erratic; this turned out to be a masterful understatement. To us, anything was better than a further protracted sojourn in Bor, so we readily accepted his terms of fare and agreed to complete the loading and lashing without worrying his crew.

After two long hours of shoving, rocking and heaving, both Rovers were bound firmly to most improbable-looking parts of the barges and, having waved farewell to our reluctant bene-factors of Bor, and the commissioner, who seemed genuinely sorry to see us go, we set off upstream, Burton roaring off from the quayside ramp to the riotous cheers of the men of Bor. All would have seemed very rosy but for the fact that, like mother, Achmad had come too.

Our intention was that Charles should hover in a series of slow loops as we progressed to the south, keeping the tug as much in sight as was conveniently possible to please the anxious Achmad. The boat was sandbagged round the wheelhouse and had a small but heavily armed Army section for an escort. The river pilot, a Dongola man from the area of Aswan who had the river in his blood and stood, as though transfixed, at the heavy teak wheel, had made the journey countless times and must have known the meandering vagaries of the river intimately.

Charles was quite prepared to take Burton on to Juba alone, but Achmad had vetoed any such plans, saying that an un-escorted night halt en route to Juba was fraught with potential danger and out of the question. The result was hilarious; a frus-trated Charles hovered hot and scowling, within a mile of the tug, buzzing the barges with increasing proximity. The guards began to throw bread and oranges and cheer encouragement as Charles induced fast skid turns with the aid of the hyacinth islands. Hippo and crocodiles appeared from time to time, and water-buck scat-tered from the banks as we approached though the hovercraft failed to move them.

The skipper sat in his wheelhouse chewing tobacco whilst the ancient river-pilot—who appeared to have an infinite capacity for accurate spitting, pointed a dirty hand to his left or right front to indicate the right direction to his little apprentice. This was very necessary, for the reeds and hyacinth obscured and confused the main waterway, especially by night, and should the wrong stream be chosen, a gnarled creature would rush from the engine-room with a sounding pole, screaming out numbers as he sounded the depths, until deep waters were again reached.

The wheelman had an exceptional method of negotiating the

river bends which nearly resulted in both our Rovers breaking their bonds and slipping from the barges. Whenever an acute bend loomed ahead, the complete unit of tug and barges was steered for the outer bank and bounced off the barrier of reeds to facilitate the turn. Sleep on the foredeck under such conditions was not easy to come by, and the counting of sheep was interrupted by mosquitoes of an alarming size which appeared in clouds at dusk and made themselves noisily evident until the following day towards dawn.

After three days of this giddy journey, which Charles estimated would have taken him less than a day in Burton had Achmad's restrictions not been applied, we drew in at Juba on the 28th; a Friday—the Prophet's holiday—which meant that everything was closed, including the Army offices and customs building.

We had been unable to send home any news of our progress from the moment we left Malakal and now found the Juba post office locked and empty and its only postbox inside the building.

The Sudan-Uganda border crossing-point is at Nimule; but all documents, vehicles and equipment have to be checked at Juba, since although it is over a hundred miles north of the Ugandan border, no transport can pass north or south without crossing on the Juba ferry. All the papers so carefully prepared by our friend Mr. Moyadeen in Wadi Halfa would have to be cleared before we could board the ferry to the east bank, where the shanty town of Gondokoro once lay. It had been important in the days when Juba was just a stretch of bushy bank and Speke, Grant and Baker had completed their explorations with this dismal area as their starting or finishing point—depending on whether they had begun their expeditions from the north or east coast of Africa.

South of Juba and until it meets the border, the river is a seething rush of turbulence—unnavigable and narrow—so that the explorers, if they had mastered the maze of the Sudd, had to moor their boats at Gondokoro, fever-ridden slaving centre though it was, before continuing overland to the region of the lakes.

At Juba there was much loading and unloading of military bric-à-brac from the ferry and from a recently built railway line to Wau in the south-western forests where most of the rebel activities were concentrated.Lithe black 'warriors' with toy pistols clambered in and out of camouflaged and amphibious armoured cars whilst their fat mamas pounded the family washing on the river-bank, their white-clad and ample posteriors bobbing in sympathy with their exertions.

The Sudan Rail storage sheds on the waterfront had their own concrete ramp which sloped gently into the water and provided an easy means of retrieving Burton from the Nile. The Land-Rovers disembarked in the no longer startling manner of driving down two thin metal ramps placed between bank and boatdeck by a party of friendly soldiers—who addressed Nick as Colonel, much to his pleasure.

Since everything was closed and the atmosphere of the place drooled drowsy somnolence, it was quite on the cards that our next step south would be no quicker than the last. It had long since become clear that no minor official in the South would take decisions without prior reference to his superior and since this attitude extended all the way up the various ladders of influence, it saved a lot of time if one could contact and gain the backing of the local Number One on arrival.

In Juba, military headquarters of Equatoria province, the lewa or major-general was the most prominent local personality and fortunately a friend of Brigadier Harrar, our Khartoum ally, from whom we had a letter of introduction.

I found a sentry post with a field telephone and, after numerous attempts, got on to the lewa's A.D.C. and told him of our arrival. His boss, Ahmed el Sherif el Habib, G.O.C. of Southern Command in Equatoria arrived that evening in an impressively signed and beflagged khaki Humber, drawing up beneath the ebony trees by our tug as though on the gravel drive of an Aldershot residence. The general was in full working regalia with the star, crossed-swords and baton of his rank, and I restrained a conditioned impulse to salute. He was a large man with a gentle voice and mannerisms and showed an intelligent interest in Burton and the journey. He was very surprised that we had been allowed through either Egypt or Khartoum and intimated that in a very short while the route might no longer be accessible to tourists. He invited us to dine with him and his chiefs of staff that night and promised that an escort with transport for Burton would be ready the next day. Even the customs official was retrieved from some downtown whisky den and opened his office—for the first time ever on a Friday, he assured us—for long enough to clear our papers. He seemed to think that we had sold Baker and both trailers to the commissioner of Bor who obviously had a reputation for fleecing passers-by. I gave him, as exactly as was possible, the locations of the abandoned trailers, and of Baker (hoping that the commissioner hadn't moved the latter to some flowery bower in his orchard) and had pleasant visions of customs inspectors touring the Mogoch area in rowing-boats with binoculars to verify my story of the trailers' fate.

A young infantry captain called at the Juba Hotel where we had been billeted, and took us to the Officers' Club—a low sprawling system of breeze-block buildings with an outside terrace. Subdued lighting flickered on glass where a sumptuous display of drink packed the bar alcove and well over a hundred officers in slacks and shirtsleeves made merry away from the front.

The severe drinking-laws of the Prophet are obviously considered null and void in times of war.

General Sherif welcomed us to his table which he shared with his aides and a young Japanese salesman selling night vision rifle sights. Johnny Walker ruled the table but a dark red wine with its label in Arabic—probably an Algerian brand—helped wash down a selection of salads and sweetmeats, including some baleful and tasteless sheep's eyes. There were no women present but the band broke into Beatles music and several 'couples' were jiving expertly to the blaring tunes of the 'Yellow Submarine'. As more officers finished their meal, one side of the terrace was cleared of tables and the dancers increased in number.

To my amazement two of the chiefs of staff paired off and settled down to an energetic twist, at which General Ahmed Sherif smiling at our obvious astonishment, suggested we also dance.

Presuming that refusal might well offend, I took to the floor with the Japanese. I couldn't make out whether he was accus-

184

tomed to such things or not since he wore a near-permanent
Oriental smirk and spoke little English and no Arabic. I found it
hard to believe that he could explain to anyone at Southern
Command Juba what a night vision rifle sight was, let alone how
it functioned. My fast-waning self-confidence returned slightly on
noticing that Nick and Charles had succumbed to the general's
pressure and were cavorting around the terrace; Nick shaking
expertly whilst Charles attempted a unique version of the
Charleston. As I thankfully subsided into my earlier chair
acknowledging the bow of the Japanese; I found it difficult to
refrain from a comment to the general on the 'Black and White
Minstrel Show'. The officers evidently considered after-dinner
stag dances to be a perfectly normal way of passing the evening,
but I noticed that the general himself was content with Johnny
Walker for a partner and an outsize Havana cigar to round off
his dinner.

Two army lorries of the usual design met us by the river the
next morning and Burton was lifted high and enthroned on one
of them to the amusement of a curious crowd of Sudan Rail
workers fresh from their Friday off.

This time we had a friendly sergeant-major to command the
escort platoon who was unconcerned about our photography.
He also shared our desire to press on; for although the forests
which spread from Juba to Nimule are well-garrisoned by army
outposts, he was uneasy making the journey with so few men.

Achmad had left us unobserved the day before and with him
went the veil of suspicion that had been with us since Khartoum.
Unfortunately, now that our cameras could click free and
unfettered, good subject-matter was scarce. For the government
had followed a ruthless scorched-earth policy in the whole region.
The rolling hill country which stretches south from Juba and
continues virtually uninterrupted through most of northern Uganda is densely wooded and slashed frequently with rocky gullies,
making it a fine place for small guerilla bands. They can ambush
convoys on the Nimule road and fade into the dense brush before
effective counter-action is mounted. When the government forces
organise large-scale cordon and sweep operations, the guerillas
find no difficulty in withdrawing down their forest routes and

185

over the border into Uganda where many thousands of their
fellow Anya Nya have already taken refuge, and from where
they can prepare for further forays without danger of surprise
and capture.

On a road such as the Nimule one, where ambush is an ever-
present and very real danger, it is an advantage for convoy
troops to be able to fire at anything that moves on sight,
without hesitating to verify whether it is innocent civilian
or would be killer—especially when both look and dress alike.
The result of this and similar lines of thought emanating from
the Military Government, had led to reports of massacres by
government troops, of starving refugees fleeing to Uganda leaving
their dead to rot and their dwellings to smoulder. Such stories
which leaked to the European press in the late nineteen-fifties
may or may not have been true. If they were, the army acted only
after considerable provocation and many losses on their own side,
for the Northerners are not by nature sadistic, even if their
history and traditions do seem barbarous.

None of the military nor civilian officials whom I consulted
had a very clear picture of what had actually happened to cause
the mass exodus from the south; or if they knew, they had
reasons for remaining silent.

Certainly major upheavals had taken place and nine years
after the probable period of events, we still saw signs of the
scars in forest clearings along the roadside. Even where
scrub and elephant-grass grew high, the scorched earth of
earlier years was noticeable. Charred wooden uprights of circular
huts were grouped in skeletal asymmetry between the frothy
leaves of acacias.

Sometimes brickwork and even complete but windowless community buildings and churches lurked quietly in the scrub some
distance from the track, decaying with their private memories
of misery and joy experienced within their walls. The whole
region has a depressing emptiness to it though its beauty cannot
be denied. Even the sight of a wayside beggar would have
cheered me up, but not a soul lived or travelled in those parts
as far as we could judge.

Game was scarce, though we had expected the area to teem

with animal life. Possibly past battles and trigger-happy convoys near the road had taught the local game to keep away. When a young buck crossed our path, the front Mercedes came to a halt and the sergeant-major with some of his men dashed off with their rifles. Minutes later they returned without the buck, but with a brace of fine partridge. The fowls were plucked during the rest of the journey affording the soldiers much amusement since a quantity of the feathers blew back and stuck to our windscreen. The men were confident enough, and evidently alert for their automatic weapons never left their grasp and they kept silent, which was surprising in any Arab force.

Twice we came upon camouflaged groups of soldiers in about company strength. I saw no officers nor were any tented camps in evidence in the deeper forest. This was not the case by the road bridges, spanning wicked-looking gorges, where amphibious vehicles and sandbagged positions kept the road open from the acts of saboteurs.

Large green snakes that seemed to prefer the hot murram road-surface as a basking area slid away with quick blurrs of powerful motion as we approached.

Dusk settled quietly as our little convoy descended the last steep pass to Nimule. Turning west from the border road we came to some barracks with many lorries and armoured cars. There was no electricity and men moved around in the darkness, our escort deserting us and their lorries with an air of finality for their kit bundles went too. I stumbled round in the dark, trying to find the sergeant-major by following the men. This was unsuccessful since they all went first to the latrines and then to a sort of mess hall where large cauldrons of steaming pottage were attacked with dipping platters. They grinned at me whilst munching happily but ignored my queries as to the where-abouts of their officers' mess. The cook corporal, a little Zanzibari with a flowing moustache, spoke American with pride and led me off to the sergeants' mess, where our sergeant-major, also dining busily, surveyed me with surprise. Why wasn't I eating or sleeping? This was Nimule—what more did I want?

I explained that two of us had planes to catch in only forty-eight hours' time from Nairobi—at least four hundred miles away. Unless we crossed the border that night, they stood no chance of catching the plane and would lose their jobs. The R.S.M. introduced himself in passable English and pointed out that Sudanese army lorries were not allowed to approach within a mile of the border under any pretext without orders from Southern Command which could not be obtained that night. I told him we had been dancing with his chiefs of staff twenty-four hours earlier and the general had even opened the customs office for us on a Friday to help speed us on our way.

After much discussion both the R.S.M. and the sergeant-major donned their bush hats, and with a platoon of grumbling soldiers back on Burton's lorry, we set off for the border—three miles to the south.

The R.S.M. halted the truck in a narrow lane and we continued with him in the Land-Rover until a striped barrier and group of whitewashed huts indicated the Ugandan border. The R.S.M. greeted a uniformed Ugandan who appeared from the shadows and, pointing at us repeatedly, explained our predicament with many resigned gestures. Certainly no money changed hands but the guard seemed to know the R.S.M. well and agreed to his request—with the result that soon afterwards a Sudanese lorry and a platoon of armed men crossed the Ugandan border at midnight on the 30th and deposited Burton onto Ugandan turf.

Realising the risk the R.S.M.—and the border guard—had taken to help us, we parted with the last of the expedition's whisky and shook the hands of the entire platoon before they withdrew to their own side of the border and disappeared.

Nick and Peter left us as soon as their papers were cleared and roared off—literally, for their silencer had dropped off—in the old diesel Land-Rover, wishing the rest of us luck with the final phase of the journey. Short of a bad breakdown they stood a reasonable chance of reaching Nairobi by 1st April when the R.A.F. had a plane leaving for Britain. A telegram we received a week later confirmed that they had caught the plane and after suffering some initial acid comments from their respective employers, had settled down to their old jobs.

The Ugandan chief customs inspector was still in bed at nine the next morning—since it was a Sunday, and Ugandans, being

Christian, worked on Fridays and rested on Sundays—but his very attractive wife was up and made us coffee while we waited. The inspector was disgruntled that his underling had allowed the diesel vehicle through without consulting him. Doubtless he would have been even more disturbed if he had been awoken and witnessed our arrival and escort. Keen to get rid of us, he soon completed our papers and assured us there were no lorries large enough to take Burton south to Kampala anywhere nearer than Gulu, at least ninety miles away.

An Indian merchant in Gulu whom we found with the help of the local police hired us an Isuzu pickup van with a driver. It was smaller than Burton but, in the absence of anything else, would have to suffice.

Back at the border, an unexpected problem—there was no-one around to lift the Hawk onto the Isuzu. The guard told us that days went by without any vehicle crossing the border, so rather than wait indefinitely, we made do with the chief customs officer, his wife and the three guards. Fortunately the van was low as well as small and after much exhortation to the guards and driver—whose efforts were directed more to studying the inspector's wife as she bent to lift the craft than to using their own considerable strength—Burton was eventually secured on planks on the Isuzu's tiny load-platform. The craft's snout protruded well over the back of the platform and the skirt hung low on either side. After lashing it securely, we left the perspiring but relieved customs officer and drove south through the banana plantations. We stopped only in the early hours of 1st April to repair a leaking water pipe on the van with a makeshift rubber sleeve ripped from Burton's skirt.

The road was of packed murram dirt which set up a fine red dust behind the Isuzu and covered the Land-Rover and us. We crossed the Karuma Falls marvelling at the immensity of the river's power as it passed beneath us in thundering spate. On to Masindi Port, through a land of forest and vivid colour where the early explorers had suffered at the hands of treacherous native kings a century ago during their search for the source which for so long eluded them.

We came to Kampala at midday and called at the British Commission to enquire where and when the hover demonstration was to be held. Having for so long planned the event, the Commercial Attaché was quite prepared to arrange it more or less at our convenience and we settled for the 3rd by when Burton could be thoroughly checked for any damage which might have occurred since leaving the Nile at Juba.

The Military Attaché and his wife were the soul of hospitality during our stay in Kampala. They had followed our progress from Cairo in the *Telegraph* and when we finally arrived on the 1st April, said they had virtually written us off as citizens of southern Sudan.

On the morning of the 3rd, Burton roared into life and sped proudly over the yacht-club lawn at Gaba onto the clear surface of Lake Victoria, to the amazement of a large gathering of businessmen and ministers from Kampala and nearby industrial Jinja. This then was the tiny craft that had come from faraway Britain to follow the course of the world's longest river, as had Baker and Burton a hundred years before. The East African press turned out in strength to witness the advent of the first hovercraft in Uganda and, as in the Sudan, agents were found on behalf of Hoverair for future sales arrangements. Our journey had ended and only months later did we realise the extent of its after-effects. The Ministry of Technology, astonished that the little craft had survived both the rigours of the journey and my own talent for trouble and was still operating perfectly, arranged a sales tour of the United States and Canada. At the time of writing, some twenty million pounds worth of export orders from these countries have been placed for Hoverair's mini-machines, craft which, like all small hovercraft, had previously suffered under the stigma of unreliability. We felt we had done our bit, albeit indirectly, for the Chancellor of the Exchequer.

We had not been able to hover up the length of the Nile, nor did the early explorers manage to follow its entire course, but we had savoured a taste of its perils, the extremes of climate and terrain through which it flows, and as we progressed along its passage, had been filled with the same desire as the explorers; to see the vast watershed where the mighty river is born. And so, standing on the grassy slopes above the Ripon Falls as twilight's silky orange touched the lake, we felt contentment, and a certain satisfaction at knowing the great river and the peoples of its lands.